Walter Scott

GATEWAY SERIES

THE LADY OF THE LAKE

BY

SIR WALTER SCOTT

EDITED BY

RAYMOND MACDONALD ALDEN, Ph.D.
PROFESSOR OF ENGLISH IN THE UNIVERSITY OF ILLINOIS

NEW YORK ·:· CINCINNATI ·:· CHICAGO

AMERICAN BOOK COMPANY

PREFACE BY THE GENERAL EDITOR

THIS series of books aims, first, to give the English texts required for entrance to college in a form which shall make them clear, interesting, and helpful to those who are beginning the study of literature; and, second, to supply the knowledge which the student needs to pass the entrance examination. For these two reasons it is called *The Gateway Series*.

The poems, plays, essays, and stories in these small volumes are treated, first of all, as works of literature, which were written to be read and enjoyed, not to be parsed and scanned and pulled to pieces. A short life of the author is given, and a portrait, in order to help the student to know the real person who wrote the book. The introduction tells what it is about, and how it was written, and where the author got the idea, and what it means. The notes at the foot of the page are simply to give the sense of the hard words so that the student can read straight on without turning to a dictionary. The other notes, at the end of the book, explain difficulties and allusions and fine points.

The editors are chosen because of their thorough training and special fitness to deal with the books committed to them, and because they agree with this idea of what a Gateway Series ought to be. They express, in each case, their own views of the books which they edit. Simplicity, thoroughness, shortness, and clearness, — these, we hope, will be the marks of the series.

HENRY VAN DYKE.

PREFACE

The Lady of the Lake should be read primarily for simple enjoyment, not for the study of history or geography. Knowledge of some historical and geographical details is, however, indispensable to the understanding of the story; these, and nothing more, it has been the aim of the editor to supply in the notes. The student may well read the poem as rapidly as he can understand it. The map forming page 36 will be found to contain nearly all the geographical names mentioned in the text, and should be constantly used in connection with the notes.

Among the many editions of *The Lady of the Lake*, that of Dr. William J. Rolfe, in the Riverside Press series, is deserving of special mention. The present editor owes acknowledgment for assistance found in Dr. Rolfe's careful work on the text of the poem, as well as in his notes on geographical details.

R. M. A.

STANFORD UNIVERSITY,
CALIFORNIA.

CONTENTS

INTRODUCTION

I. LIFE AND CHARACTER OF SCOTT

THE author of *The Lady of the Lake* and the Waverley Novels is one of the most agreeable figures one can meet in making the acquaintance of the great names in our literature. He did not conceal his own personality behind his work, like Shakespeare and other dramatic poets, but showed his hearty and kindly nature in all that he wrote ; and he lived among friends who appreciated the importance of his work, so that we have in their records of his life and character as full an account of Scott as we could wish for. Indeed, the biography written by John G. Lockhart, his son-in-law, is commonly considered one of the best two biographies in the English language — Boswell's *Life of Johnson* being the other. Every reader of Scott will wish sooner or later to make his acquaintance through this book ; for the present purpose we need only look rapidly at the outlines of his life, drawing upon Lockhart, of course, for most of the material.

Walter Scott was the son of an Edinburgh lawyer, and was born in the Scotch capital on August 15, 1771. As a boy he was a bright, active youngster, entering heartily into all sports and outdoor exercises, in spite of the fact that from infancy he suffered from a lameness in one leg. The cheerfulness with which he met and largely overcame the disadvantages of this trouble, and the frankness with which he always spoke of it, contrast pleasantly with the sensitiveness and morbid regrets always shown by Lord Byron in connexion with his similar deformity.

In his studies Scott did not especially distinguish himself, but he was always passionately fond of literature and history, and had an extraordinary memory which all through life enabled him to repeat, almost word for word, any part of his reading in which he had been particularly interested. An amusing story is told of him when only six years old, that he said to his aunt that he liked a certain Mrs. Cockburn who had been visiting the family, because she was *a virtuoso like himself.* "Walter," said his Aunt Jenny, "what is a virtuoso?" "Why, it's one who wishes and will know everything." Another noticeable fact about his childhood was his fondness for the old Scotch and English ballads, especially those telling of the warring days of the "Border chivalry." Over these he would pore by the hour, and by the time he was twelve years old he had a collection of them, many of which he had picked up in pamphlet form at book-shops, amounting to several volumes. He has himself told us of the day when he first came across the *Reliques of Ancient Poetry*, edited by Dr. Percy, — the chief collection of the old ballads made in the eighteenth century. "I remember well the spot where I read these volumes for the first

time. It was beneath a huge platanus tree, in the ruins
of what had been intended for an old-fashioned arbour in
the garden I have mentioned. The summer day sped
onward so fast that, notwithstanding the sharp appetite
of thirteen, I forgot the hour of dinner, was sought for
with anxiety, and was still found entranced in my intel-
lectual banquet. . . . Henceforth I overwhelmed my
schoolfellows, and all who would hearken to me, with
tragical recitations from the ballads." The importance
of this lies in the fact that it was these old ballad stories
which formed in a sense the models for Scott's poems of
adventure.

In like manner the romantic scenery of the Scotch
lakes and mountains was full of poetic and historic interest for him. When he was taken to visit any of the bits
of interesting country within easy reach of Edinburgh, he
not only enjoyed its natural beauty for its own sake, but
filled it in with the imaginary forms of the monks and
knights, the fair ladies and the warriors, of the age of
romance. Speaking again of the time when he was twelve
or thirteen years old, he tells how his "romantic feelings"
connected themselves with the landscape ; "and the historical incidents, or traditional legends connected with
many of them, gave to my admiration a sort of intense
impression of reverence, which at times made my heart
feel too big for its bosom. From this time the love of
natural beauty, more especially when combined with
ancient ruins, or remains of our fathers' piety or splen-
dour, became with me an insatiable passion."

And when he could not be in the country, or even in out-door sports, his imagination still did him good service. At the age of sixteen he was confined to his room by a long illness, and he relates how one of his amusements during this time was to call to mind the wars and battles of which he had read in history. These he worked out by the " expedient of arranging shells, and seeds, and pebbles, so as to represent encountering armies. Diminutive crossbows were contrived to mimic artillery, and with the assistance of a friendly carpenter I contrived to model a fortress, which . . . represented whatever place happened to be uppermost in my imagination. I fought my way thus through Vertot's *Knights of Malta*, a book which, as it hovered between history and romance, was exceedingly dear to me." All through life Scott kept up his interest in military matters, and for a great part of his early manhood he was officer of a volunteer troop of cavalry in which his good horsemanship gave him a prominent place, despite his lameness. One result of all this is that his writings excel in descriptions of military affairs, his battles — whether in prose or verse — being among the liveliest and at the same time the clearest in literature.

When he came of age, without waiting to complete a university course, Scott was admitted to the bar and began to practise law in his father's office and for himself. But while he was by no means a failure in this profession, he did not especially distinguish himself in it, and soon came to have more interest in literature. After a few years, when his success in poetry had — as he expressed it — made people suspicious of his qualities as a man of affairs, he quite abandoned the practice of his profession ; but in 1799 he was made sheriff of Selkirk-shire, and in 1806 one of the clerks of the Court of Session at Edinburgh — positions which he held for nearly the whole of his remaining life.   For these offices, which brought him some £1600 ($8000) a year, his legal training, of course, stood him in good stead ; it also furnished him no little useful material for his novels.

Meantime, at the close of the year 1797, Scott was married.   His first love had been a certain Williamina Stuart, whose family was considered to be above the rank of Scott's, so that the parents of both the young people appear to have thought the match undesirable.   Miss Stuart eventually married a gentleman (later a baronet) who became a fast friend of Scott's.   In the same year in which she was married, Scott met Miss Charlotte Charpentier, or Carpenter, the daughter of a French Protestant refugee.   "A lovelier vision," says Lockhart, " as all who remember her in the bloom of her days have assured me, could hardly have been imagined ; and from that hour the fate of the young poet was fixed."   But notwithstanding the genuineness of his devotion to the lady who soon became his wife, Scott regarded it as something less passionate than that which he had felt during his " three years of dreaming " of Williamina Stuart.   Long after his marriage he wrote to a friend : " Mrs. Scott's match and mine was of our own making, and proceeded from the most sincere affection on both sides, which has rather increased than diminished during twelve years' marriage. But it was something short of love in all its forms, which I suspect people only *feel* once in their lives." Mrs. Scott does not appear to have had a strong imagination or any unusual interest in literature ; hence she could not exert such an influence on her husband's work as the wives of some other poets have done. But she was a thoroughly good wife and mother, and when she died, in 1826, Scott wrote in his diary, "I wonder how I shall do with the large portion of thoughts which were hers for thirty years."

Four children came to the household, two boys (Walter and Charles) and two girls (Sophia and Anne). The many pictures which we get of the family life while all were still together at home are almost without exception pleasant ones ; and Scott's letters to his sons, written after they went away from home to study, are those of a father both wise and kind, who made his children his companions. The older son entered the army, and the younger the government civil service. Sophia married John Lockhart, one of the rising young literary men whom Scott had befriended ; while his other daughter, Anne, remained his constant companion until his death. None of the children survived their father by many years.

Turning back now to trace Scott's literary work, we find that his earliest published poems were translations of some German ballads, which he had made for his own amusement. Later he wrote original verses of the same general character ; and in the meantime his continued studies in the ballad literature of his own country gradually led to the book called *Minstrelsy of the Scottish Border*, which he published in 1802. In this work Scott included not only the popular ballads which he had gathered from many sources, but also modern imitations of them by a few of his friends and by himself; and his first important and celebrated poem, the *Lay of the Last Minstrel*, was originally intended for a place in the same collection, but grew in his hands until it seemed better suited to form a book by itself. It appeared in January, 1805, and was so well received that, as Lockhart tells us, "its success at once decided that literature should form the main business of Scott's life." The first edition consisted only of 750 copies, the second of 1500, the third, fourth, and fifth of about 2000 each; and before Scott collected his poems, twenty-five years later, more than 40,000 copies of the *Lay* had been sold in Great Britain alone. The story of the success of the poems that followed is almost the same. For *Marmion*, published in 1808, the publishers offered £1000 without having seen a line of it, — or, as Byron said, "just half a crown per line." The principal poems that followed were *The Lady of the Lake*, in 1810; *Rokeby*, in 1812; *The Bridal of Triermain*, in 1813; *The Lord of the Isles*, in 1815, and *Harold the Dauntless*, in 1817.

In 1813 Scott was asked by the Prince Regent to become Poet Laureate, in recognition of his being the most popular poet in the kingdom; but he declined the honour, and managed to secure it for his friend, Robert

Southey, who needed the salary more than he. This period marks the turning-point from the part of Scott's life which was devoted chiefly to poetry, to that which was devoted to prose romances. In 1813 Lord Byron published two of his metrical romances, *The Giaour* and *The Bride of Abydos*, and among London readers his fame was beginning to outshine Scott's. Although Byron sent to the elder poet a copy of *The Giaour* with the inscription, "To the Monarch of Parnassus from one of his subjects," Scott was nevertheless one of the first to see that his genius in poetry was not the equal of Byron's. "He hits the mark where I don't even pretend to fledge my arrow," he said to one of his intimate friends ; and long afterward, near the close of his life, he said that one reason why he had given up poetry was because Byron, who had a deeper knowledge of the human heart, was taking his place. In the same year, 1813, Scott set to work on his first novel, *Waverley*, which he had begun some years before and abandoned ; and in 1814 it was published. Thus began the second and more brilliant period of his literary career.

Into the details of this new period we need not at present go. Even the list of Scott's romances is too long to repeat here, and the story of their success belongs to the study of his work in prose. They followed one another with extraordinary rapidity, and were even more eagerly bought and read than the poems had been. Between 1814 and 1825 Scott had written more than twenty of these books, and had received for them more than £25,000. Part of this money was spent in providing for his children; a part was invested in the printing establishment of his friends, the Ballantynes, who had made their reputation by printing his works; but the greater part was devoted to building up his estate of Abbotsford, where this, the happiest period of his life, was largely spent.

Abbotsford was in Scott's favourite Border country, south of Edinburgh, on the banks of the Tweed, and looking across the river to the Cheviot Hills of England. It had been a part of the old estate of the monks of Melrose Abbey, the ruins of which are still well preserved, and for which Scott showed a passionate devotion. His estate was at first a mere farm, but he added to it until it reached quite lordly proportions, and at the same time planned the fine residence, every nook and corner of which is associated with his care and taste, and which is still visited by countless pilgrims who honour his memory. His official duties called him to Edinburgh for certain months of each year, but the moment he could leave them he would hasten back to Abbotsford, to his beloved river and trees, his horses and dogs. Here he entertained, with splendid hospitality, both friends from every quarter of Great Britain and visitors of more or less distinction from all over the world. Every visitor of this sort who made any record of his experiences at Abbotsford has recorded the kindness and grace which Scott showed as a host, and the simplicity and charm of his home life. His time seemed always at the disposal of his family and friends, though in reality he was usually careful to save a part of each morning for rapid work at his desk. Scott's novels had all been published without the author's name, and the secret of the authorship was revealed only to a few of his most intimate friends, though it gradually came to be understood by all who knew him. But he never permitted any personal conversation on the subject, and his family laughingly accepted the popular phrase and called him "the Great Unknown." So he led a simpler life than would have been possible if he had become the acknowledged leading novelist of Great Britain; and there were even some of his friends to whom it seemed impossible that the man who was always at leisure for riding, hunting, telling stories, corresponding with his friends, or doing a service for any one in need, could be at the same time the writer of two three-volume novels in a year.

In 1825, five years after he had been made a baronet by the personal choice of the king, this happy period of Scott's life came to a close through the loss of his fortune. It was the investment in the Ballantyne printing house which brought the crash. Neither the Ballantynes nor Scott had given sufficient attention to the details of business, and when some of the firms with which theirs was connected fell into difficulties at this time, they were found to be so involved that there was no possibility of avoiding a failure. Their debts all told amounted to over £110,000, or considerably more than half a million of dollars, and the honour of Scott was involved in them all.

Lord Cockburn, a prominent Scotchman of this period, has recorded the impression made on the community by Scott's misfortune. "The opening of the year 1826 will ever be sad to those who remember the thunderbolt which then fell on Edinburgh in the utterly unexpected bankruptcy of Scott. . . . If an earthquake had swallowed half the town, it would not have produced greater astonishment, sorrow, and dismay. . . . How humbled we felt when we saw him — the pride of us all, dashed from his lofty and honourable station, and all the fruits of his well-worked talents gone. . . . Well do I remember his first appearance after this calamity was divulged, when he walked into court one day in January, 1826. There was no affectation, and no reality, of facing it; no look of indifference or defiance; but the manly and modest air of a gentleman conscious of some folly, but of perfect rectitude, and of most heroic and honourable resolutions. It was on that very day, I believe, that he said a very fine thing. Some of his friends offered him, or rather proposed to offer him, enough of money, as was supposed, to enable him to arrange with his creditors. He paused for a moment; and then, recollecting his powers, said proudly, ' No ! this right hand shall work it all off !' "

The remaining years of his life were spent in fulfilling this resolution. Scott believed that if his strength should last long enough, and his popularity as a novelist continue, he could write books which would enable him to pay all that he owed. But he was now more than fifty years old, and the task was too heavy. He did accomplish wonders, paying from the profits of his writings nearly half the debt of the firm with which he had been associated, in only five years' time. But his work, which had formerly been only a pleasure to him, now became a burden. His strength and buoyancy gave way, and at length a stroke of paralysis left him comparatively helpless in both body and mind. A journey to the Mediterranean was planned for the benefit of his health, and the esteem in which he was held is strikingly shown by the fact that his Majesty's government set apart a frigate of the navy for Sir Walter's use. But he continued to fail, and was eager to return to his beloved Abbotsford to die. When quite near the end he sent for his son-in-law, Mr. Lockhart, and said to him: "Lockhart, I may have but a minute to speak to you. My dear, be a good man — be virtuous — be religious — be a good man. Nothing else will give you any comfort when you come to lie here." On the 21st of September, 1832, as Lockhart tells us, "Sir Walter breathed his last, in the presence of all his children. It was a beautiful day — so warm that every window was wide open — and so perfectly still that the sound of all others most delicious to his ear, the gentle ripple of the Tweed over its pebbles, was distinctly audible as we knelt around the bed."

It was peculiarly true of Scott that "none knew him but to love him." The pleasure that he had given by his writings was so great that, as the Earl of Dudley said at the time of his financial misfortunes, " Let every man to whom he has given months of delight give him a six-pence, and he will rise to-morrow morning richer than Rothschild ! " But this was not all. Other great writers, like Pope, Burns, Coleridge, Byron, and Carlyle, have given pleasure to thousands of readers, but their readers have nevertheless been unable to forget important defects in their character. Those who knew Scott most intimately saw no such spots on his fame. He was a perfect gentle-man, and there is hardly a recorded instance of his lower-ing his own standard of character or doing an unkind-ness. His age was, unfortunately, one of literary quarrels ; but Scott was the friend of every other poet of his time, and never quarrelled with any of them, even under provo-cation. He firmly believed in the law of kindness. In his last years, looking back over his career and speaking of some of his critics, he wrote : " I let parody, burlesque, and squibs find their own level ; and while the latter hissed most fiercely, I was cautious never to catch them up, as school-boys do, to throw them back against the naughty boy who fired them off, wisely remembering that they are in such cases apt to explode in the handling." His only warm disputes were on political matters, for he was an ardent Tory, and honestly opposed the opposite party whenever there was occasion. But he did this in such good spirit that Lord Cockburn observed that at the time of his failure there was not one of his political op-ponents " who would not have given every spare farthing he possessed to relieve Sir Walter." The kindliness and pure-heartedness, then, which appear in his writings are the revelation of the man himself.

In a sense Scott always remained boyish. Once, in writing to a lady who knew him only by correspondence, he said: "I am afraid you have formed a higher opinion of me than I deserve: you would expect to see a person who had dedicated himself much to literary pursuits, and you would find me a rattle-skulled half-lawyer, half-sportsman, through whose head a regiment of horse has been exercising since he was five years old; half-educated — half-crazy, as his friends sometimes tell him." So he never lost his love for his horses and dogs, for games and hunting, for stories of war and romance. He always kept, too, a fondness for a certain sort of aristocratic display, which was at the same time not inconsistent with simplicity of spirit. He liked processions and ceremonials; he was careful to observe the old festivals of Scottish life as they came around from year to year; he genuinely enjoyed the right to emblazon his coat-of-arms as a baronet; and one of his greatest pleasures in building up his Abbotsford estate was in gathering around him tenants and servants who would be devoted to him, and to whom he would show kindness, in the old-fashioned position of a lord of the manor. It was natural, then, that he should not be of a temper to sympathize with the growth of democratic ideas which tended to break down all political and social distinctions between men; and it is perhaps the chief limitation of Scott that he failed to understand or sympathize with the reform movements of his time. In the same way we do not find in either his poetry or his novels any traces of the influence of modern democratic ideas, but rather the atmosphere of the earlier days when all well-disposed people were content with things as they found them.

Scott preferred to think of himself as a gentleman and an active man of the world, who wrote poetry for the pleasure of it and for the sake of making a little additional pocket-money, rather than as a man of letters. "Did any of my sons," he once wrote, "show poetical talent, of which, to my great satisfaction, there are no appearances, the first thing I should do would be to inculcate upon him the duty of cultivating some honourable profession, and qualifying himself to play a more respectable part in society than the mere poet." And in another letter : "'I had rather be a kitten and cry mew'" (quoting Shakespeare), "than write the best poetry in the world on condition of laying aside common sense in the ordinary transactions and business of the world." Now from one point of view this feeling was, of course, very sensible, and preserved Scott from the affectations and conceits of small men of letters ; but it is easy to see, on the other hand, that it shows a lower view of poetry than the greater poets have taken. We can imagine Wordsworth, or Shelley, or Tennyson indignant enough at the expression "the mere poet." To them the poet was the truest teacher of his age, with powers and duties as sacred as those of a king, a priest, or a prophet. Here again, then, we find a limitation of

Scott's. He lived largely in the material world, and wrote of solid men and things, rather than of spiritual forces or moral ideals, although he thoroughly believed in these also. He was right in saying that his poetry must take a second place; for it is not of the sort that reveals great truths, expresses great ideas and profound passions, or leads men into higher living.

But it does not follow that his poetry is to be despised. He used it for the same purpose which he afterwards decided he could accomplish better in prose, — that of telling wholesome and brilliant stories in a way that makes them live in our imaginations. He delighted to bring back the earlier days, "the age of romance," in all the fascination which it had for him when as a boy his fancy brought back the old warring chieftains to the glens of the Highlands, the monks to the ruins of Melrose Abbey, and armoured knights to the castles of Tantallon or Stirling. His life, he said near its close, had been a sort of dream. "I have worn a wishing-cap, the power of which has been to divert present griefs by a touch of the wand of imagination, and gild over the future by prospects more fair than can be realized." This wonderful wishing-cap and this magic wand he has handed down to all his readers. One of his admirers early called him "the Great Magician," and the title will always be associated with his memory. We go to him, as his own children used to gather around his chair in the twilight, for stories that shall make us forget ourselves in the sorrows and joys of other days.

II. The Lady of the Lake

When Scott was only about sixteen years of age, and was working in a lawyer's office, he was sent on an expedition to the Highlands, with a sergeant and six soldiers to aid him in the execution of a legal paper. "Thus it happened," as he afterwards wrote, "that the author first entered the romantic scenery of Loch Katrine, of which he may perhaps say he has somewhat extended the reputation, riding in all the dignity of danger, with a front and rear guard, and loaded arms." This was the wild country to the northwest of Edinburgh, still largely inhabited by the Celtic clans who considered themselves the original and rightful inhabitants of Scotland, and whose haunts and habits are described in both *The Lady of the Lake* and the novel *Rob Roy*. Scott often revisited the Highlands, and after the success of his earlier poems, particularly *Marmion*, he turned to the Loch Katrine region as the scene of his next work. "The scenery of Loch Katrine," he said, "was connected with the recollection of many a dear friend and merry expedition of former days. This poem, the action of which lay among scenes so beautiful and so deeply imprinted on my recollections, was a labour of love, and it was no less so to recall the manners and customs introduced."

The historical basis of *The Lady of the Lake* was found in the reign of King James V of Scotland, who became the father of Mary Queen of Scots, and who had inherited the throne when only a year old, in 1513. This year 1513 was the date of the battle of Flodden Field, which is described at the close of the story of Marmion; so that *The Lady of the Lake* follows *Marmion* in the time of its story as well as in the time of its writing. Later, in the *Tales of a Grandfather*, Scott described the reign of James V, and we can see in his narrative the facts which suggested the plot of the poem.

During his boyhood, King James was for some time under the control of Douglas, the Earl of Angus, who had married his mother; but he resented this bitterly, and at the age of sixteen escaped to the royal castle of Stirling. Then, getting the power into his own hands, he exiled the entire Douglas family, and persuaded Parliament to declare their estates forfeit. He persevered in his hatred of the Douglases, as Scott relates, "even under circumstances which rendered his unrelenting resentment ungenerous. Archibald Douglas of Kilspindie, the Earl of Angus's uncle, had been a personal favourite of the king before the disgrace of his family. He was so much recommended to James by his great strength, manly appearance, and skill in every kind of warlike exercise, that he was wont to call him his 'Graysteil,' after the name of a champion in a romance then popular. Archibald, becoming rather an old man, and tired of his exile in England, resolved to try the king's mercy. He thought that as they had been so well acquainted formerly, and as he had never offended James personally, he might find favour from their old intimacy. He therefore threw himself in the king's way one day as he returned from hunting in the park at Stirling. It was several years since James had seen him, but he knew him at a great distance, by his firm and stately step, and said, 'Yonder is my Graysteil, Archibald of Kilspindie.' But when they met, he showed no appearance of recognizing his old servant." While the Douglas of *The Lady of the Lake* is an imaginary person, this "Graysteil" forms the historical basis for his character.

Two other characteristic facts connected with James V were used by Scott in planning his poem : the warfare which the king waged against the wild freebooting chiefs of the Highlands and the Border, of whom Roderick Dhu is an imaginary type ; and his habit of going about in disguise, either for purposes of pleasure or to observe the conditions of his kingdom unsuspected. An instance of this latter sort, including one circumstance which is used in the story of Ellen's recognition of the king, Scott also related in the *Tales of a Grandfather*.

" Upon another occasion, King James, being alone and in disguise, fell into a quarrel with some gipsies, or other vagrants, and was assaulted by four or five of them. . . . There was a poor man thrashing corn in a barn near by, who came out on hearing the noise of the scuffle, and seeing one man defending himself against numbers, gallantly took the king's part with his flail, to such good purpose that the gipsies were obliged to fly. The husbandman then took the king into the barn, brought him a towel and water to wash the blood from his face and hands, and finally walked with him a little way toward

Edinburgh, in case he should be again attacked. **On the way**, the king asked his companion what and who he was. The labourer answered that his name was John Howieson, and that he was a bondsman on the farm of Braehead, near Cramond, which belonged to the king of Scotland. James then asked the poor man if there was any wish in the world which he would particularly desire should be gratified; and honest John confessed he should think himself the happiest man in Scotland were he but proprietor of the farm on which he wrought as a labourer. He then asked the king, in turn, who *he* was; and James replied, as usual, that he was the Goodman of Ballengiech, a poor man who had a small appointment about the palace; but he added that if John Howieson would come to see him on the next Sunday, he would endeavour to repay his manful assistance, and at least give him the pleasure of seeing the royal apartments. John put on his best clothes, as you may suppose, and, appearing at the postern gate of the palace, inquired for the Goodman of Ballengiech. The king had given orders that he should be admitted; and John found his friend, the goodman, in the same disguise which he had formerly worn. The king, still preserving the character of an inferior officer of the household, conducted John Howieson from one apartment of the palace to another, and was amused with his wonder and his remarks. At length James asked his visitor if he should like to see the king; to which John replied, nothing would delight him so much, if he could do so without giving offence. The Goodman of Ballengiech of course undertook that the king would not be angry. 'But,' said John, 'how am I to know his Grace from the nobles who will be all about him?' 'Easily,' replied his companion; 'all the others will be uncovered. The king alone will wear his hat or bonnet.' So speaking, King James introduced the countryman into a great hall, which was filled by the nobility and officers of the crown. John was a little frightened, and drew close to his attendant; but was still unable to distinguish the king. 'I told you that you should know him by his wearing his hat,' said the conductor. 'Then,' said John, after he had again looked round the room, 'it must be either you or me, for all but us two are bareheaded.' The king laughed at John's fancy; and that the good yeoman might have occasion for mirth also, he made him a present of the farm of Braehead, which he had wished so much to possess, on condition that John Howieson, or his successors, should be ready to present a ewer and basin for the king to wash his hands, when his Majesty should come to Holyrood palace, or should pass the bridge of Cramond."

We see, then, how the poet, finding suggestions in such historical situations as that just described, wove into them the story of the Lady of the Lake, adding the characters of Ellen Douglas and her lover, and repeopling the glens of the Highlands with warriors, as he had always been in the habit of doing, for his own pleasure, with scenes of historic interest. "I took uncommon pains," he said afterward, "to verify the accuracy of the local

circumstances of this story. I recollect in particular
that to ascertain whether I was telling a probable tale, I
went into Perthshire, to see whether King James could
actually have ridden from the banks of Loch Vennachar
to Stirling Castle within the time supposed in the poem,
and had the pleasure to satisfy myself that it was quite
practicable."

Scott also relates how he read the manuscript of the
poem to a friend, — a farmer and hunter rather than a
man of letters, — in order to test its effectiveness. "He
placed his hand across his brow, and listened with great
attention through the whole account of the stag-hunt, till
the dogs threw themselves into the lake to follow their
master, who embarks with Ellen Douglas. He then
started up with a sudden exclamation, struck his hand
on the table, and declared . . . that the dogs must have
been totally ruined by being permitted to take the water
after such a severe chase. I own I was much encour-
aged by the species of revery which had possessed so
zealous a follower of the sports of the ancient Nimrod
who had been completely surprised out of all doubts of
the reality of the tale."

In 1810, then, *The Lady of the Lake* was published.
"I do not recollect," said Mr. Cadell, an Edinburgh
gentleman of the period, "that any of all the author's
works was ever looked for with more intense anxiety,
or that any one of them excited a more extraordinary
sensation when it did appear. The whole country rang
with the praises of the poet — crowds set off to view the

scenery of Loch Katrine, till then comparatively un-known; and as the book came out just before the season for excursions, every house and inn in that neighbourhood was crammed with a constant succession of visitors."

This popularity has continued quite to our own time. Lockhart thought that, while *Marmion* might be consid-ered "the most powerful and splendid" of Scott's poems, *The Lady of the Lake* was "the most interesting, roman-tic, picturesque, and graceful." Scott himself regarded *Marmion* as being distinguished for its descriptive power, *The Lady of the Lake* for its incidents. But the fact is that it is the splendid movement of the story which gives life to both poems, as to most of his works. Whether it is the hunting of the stag, the wonderful "speeding of the cross," the battle in the Trosachs, the single combat at Coilantogle Ford, or the games at Stirling, we follow the rapid, sure-footed movements of the poet like riders on horseback dashing after an intrepid leader. The details of style or verse may sometimes be careless enough, but the story never flags.

Scott clearly recognized the real nature of his powers. He spoke of the "false gallop" of his verse, not claiming for it the subtle harmonies of the master poets, and he said that his gift was to present the "picturesque in *action*" rather than in scenery. Yet his sense of the pic-turesque in scenery was by no means slight, as *The Lady of the Lake* itself sufficiently proves. The poem has be-come the lasting guide-book to the lake region of the Scottish Highlands, and the guide not only to its geographical details but to their significance and beauty. To read it aright, then, one must have in mind this Highland region, its extent, divisions, and scenery.

The whole district that is of interest to readers of *The Lady of the Lake* seems surprisingly small to readers familiar with American distances : it covers an area extending about fifteen miles to the north and south, and twenty-five to the east and west. At the southeast corner is Stirling, with its ancient castle ; Loch Lomond lies along the western edge, with the mountain Ben Lomond rising from its eastern shore ; while through the centre of the district runs the chain composed of three lakes (Katrine, Achray, and Vennachar) and the river Teith. On all sides of these lakes are the peaks, forests, and glens of the Highlands. For our purpose two spots in the region stand out as of special interest. One of them is Coilantogle Ford, at the eastern end of Loch Vennachar, the scene of the brilliant combat of Fitz-James and Roderick Dhu. The other, even more romantic in interest, is the eastern end of Loch Katrine, the very heart of the country of *The Lady of the Lake*.

Standing at this end of the lake, one is overshadowed by the peak of Benvenue rising from its southern shore, — a peak which, although not lofty as mountain heights go in other lands, is likely to be partly shut out from view by drifting clouds and morning mists. Under its shadow, and seemingly within stone's throw of the shore, is the tiny island which Scott conceived to have been the temporary home of the Douglases, provided for them by

Roderick in the heart of his dominions, and which has
ever since gone by the name of " Ellen's Isle." To the
left the path turns upward into the forest, and is soon
winding through the wooded glen, with its mountain walls
rising on each side, to which the mountaineers gave the
name of " the Trosachs" or " bristling pass." Nowadays
there is nothing to be heard here but the rustle of the
leaves, the songs of birds, and occasionally the voices of
a party of tourists coming through by coach from Loch
Katrine to Aberfoyle or Callander ; but one is tempted
to look warily behind trees, and to watch the turn of the
road, for it was hereabouts that

> "through copse and heath arose
> Bonnets and spears and bended bows,"

and the imaginative wanderer almost wishes for a glimpse
of one of " Clan-Alpine's warriors true." It is hard to
realize that four hundred years have passed since King
James's men and those of the Highland chieftain fought
and bled here in the " Trosachs' dread defile," or since
Ellen pushed her little shallop across the lake ; yes, and
a hundred years even since Walter Scott was here tracing
out the lines of the poem. So it is that the poets keep
the old world always young for us, and make the lovers
and soldiers of long ago our never failing friends.

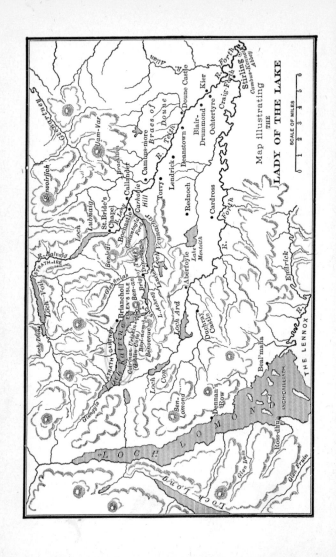

Map illustrating
THE
LADY OF THE LAKE

SCALE OF MILES
0 1 2 3 4 5 6

THE LADY OF THE LAKE

CANTO FIRST

THE CHASE

HARP of the North! that mouldering long hast hung
  On the witch-elm that shades Saint Fillan's spring,
And down the fitful breeze thy numbers[1] flung,
  Till envious ivy did around thee cling,
Muffling with verdant ringlet every string, —   5
  O minstrel Harp! still must thine accents sleep?
Mid rustling leaves and fountain's murmuring,
  Still must thy sweeter sounds their silence keep,
Nor bid a warrior smile, nor teach a maid to weep?

Not thus, in ancient days of Caledon,[2]   10
  Was thy voice mute amid the festal crowd,
When lay of hopeless love, or glory won,
  Aroused the fearful, or subdued the proud.
At each according pause, was heard aloud
  Thine ardent symphony sublime and high!   15
Fair dames and crested chiefs attention bowed;
  For still[3] the burden of thy minstrelsy
Was Knighthood's dauntless deed, and Beauty's match-
    less eye.

---

[1] Musical measures.   [2] Scotland.   [3] Always.

O wake once more! how rude soe'er the hand
　That ventures o'er thy magic maze to stray; 20
O wake once more! though scarce my skill command
　Some feeble echoing of thine earlier lay: *song*
Though harsh and faint, and soon to die away,
　And all unworthy of thy nobler strain,
Yet if one heart throb higher at its sway, 25
　The wizard note has not been touched in vain.
Then silent be no more! Enchantress, wake again!

I

THE stag at eve had drunk his fill,
Where danced the moon on Monan's rill,
And deep his midnight lair had made 30
In lone Glenartney's hazel shade;
But, when the sun his beacon red
Had kindled on Benvoirlich's head,
The deep-mouthed bloodhound's heavy bay *bark*
Resounded up the rocky way, 35
And faint, from farther distance borne,
Were heard the clanging hoof and horn.

II

As chief, who hears his warder call, *WATCHMAN*
'To arms! the foemen storm the wall,'
The antlered monarch of the waste [1] 40
Sprung from his heathery couch in haste.

[1] Wilderness.

But, ere his fleet career he took,
The dew-drops from his flanks he shook;
Like crested leader proud and high,
Tossed his beamed frontlet [1] to the sky;   45
A moment gazed adown the dale,
A moment snuffed the tainted gale,
A moment listened to the cry
That thickened as the chase drew nigh;
Then, as the headmost foes appeared,   50
With one brave bound the copse he cleared,
And, stretching forward free and far,
Sought the wild heaths of Uam-Var.

III

Yelled on the view the opening pack;
Rock, glen, and cavern paid them back;   55
To many a mingled sound at once
The awakened mountain gave response.
A hundred dogs bayed deep and strong,
Clattered a hundred steeds along,
Their peal the merry horns rung out,   60
A hundred voices joined the shout;
With hark and whoop and wild halloo,
No rest Benvoirlich's echoes knew.
Far from the tumult fled the roe,
Close in her covert cowered the doe,   65
The falcon, from her cairn [2] on high,
Cast on the rout [3] a wondering eye,

---

[1] Antlered forehead.   [2] Rocky heap.   [3] Company.

'Till far beyond her piercing ken *understanding*
The hurricane had swept the glen.
Faint and more faint, its failing din *noise*   70
Returned from cavern, cliff, and linn,[1]
And silence settled, wide and still,
On the lone wood and mighty hill.

IV

Less loud the sounds of sylvan war *grove*
Disturbed the heights of Uam-Var,   75
And roused the cavern, where, 'tis told, *hollow*
A giant made his den of old;
For ere that steep ascent was won,
High in his pathway hung the sun,
And many a gallant, stayed perforce,[2]   80
Was fain to breathe his faltering horse,
And of the trackers of the deer
Scarce half the lessening pack was near;
So shrewdly[3] on the mountain-side *sorrow*
Had the bold burst their mettle tried.   85

V

The noble stag was pausing now
Upon the mountain's southern brow,
Where broad extended, far beneath,
The varied realms of fair Menteith.
With anxious eye he wandered o'er   90
Mountain and meadow, moss and moor,

[1] Ravine.   [2] By necessity.   [3] Severely.

And ponder'd refuge from his toil,
By far Lochard or Aberfoyle.
But nearer was the copsewood[1] grey
That waved and wept on Loch Achray,   95
And mingled with the pine-trees blue
On the bold cliffs of Benvenue.
Fresh vigour with the hope returned;
With flying foot the heath he spurned,
Held westward with unwearied race,   100
And left behind the panting chase.

VI

'Twere long to tell what steeds gave o'er,
As swept the hunt through Cambus-more;
What reins were tightened in despair,
When rose Benledi's ridge in air;   105
Who flagged upon Bochastle's heath,
Who shunned to stem the flooded Teith, —
For twice that day, from shore to shore,
The gallant stag swam stoutly o'er.
Few were the stragglers, following far,   110
That reached the lake of Vennachar;
And when the Brigg of Turk was won,
The headmost horseman rode alone.

VII

Alone, but with unbated[2] zeal,
That horseman plied the scourge and steel;   115

[1] Growth of shrubs or bushes.   [2] Undiminished.

For jaded now, and spent with toil,
Embossed with foam,[1] and dark with soil,
While every gasp with sobs he drew,
The labouring stag strained full in view.
Two dogs of black Saint Hubert's breed,   120
Unmatched for courage, breath, and speed,
Fast on his flying traces came,
And all but won that desperate game;
For, scarce a spear's length from his haunch,
Vindictive toiled the bloodhounds staunch;   125
Nor nearer might the dogs attain,
Nor farther might the quarry[2] strain.
Thus up the margin of the lake,
Between the precipice and brake,
O'er stock[3] and rock their race they take.   130

VIII

The hunter marked that mountain high,
The lone lake's western boundary,
And deemed the stag must turn to bay,
Where that huge rampart barr'd the way;
Already glorying in the prize,   135
Measured his antlers with his eyes;
For the death-wound and death-halloo
Mustered his breath, his whinyard[4] drew; —
But thundering as he came prepared,

---

[1] Foaming with exhaustion.   [2] Hunted animal.   [3] Stump.
[4] Knife.

With ready arm and weapon bared, 140
The wily quarry shunned the shock,
And turned him from the opposing rock;
Then, dashing down a darksome glen,
Soon lost to hound and hunter's ken,
In the deep Trosachs' wildest nook 145
His solitary refuge took.
There, while close couched, the thicket shed
Cold dews and wild-flowers on his head,
He heard the baffled dogs in vain
Rave through the hollow pass amain, 150
Chiding the rocks that yelled again.

IX

Close on the hounds the hunter came,
To cheer them on the vanished game;
But, stumbling in the rugged dell,
The gallant horse exhausted fell. 155
The impatient rider strove in vain
To rouse him with the spur and rein,
For the good steed, his labours o'er,
Stretched his stiff limbs, to rise no more;
Then, touched with pity and remorse, 160
He sorrowed o'er the expiring horse.
' I little thought, when first thy rein
I slacked upon the banks of Seine,
That Highland eagle e'er should feed
On thy fleet limbs, my matchless steed! 165

Woe worth [1] the chase, woe worth the day,
That costs thy life, my gallant grey!'

X

Then through the dell his horn resounds,
From vain pursuit to call the hounds.
Back limped, with slow and crippled pace,   170
The sulky leaders of the chase;
Close to their master's side they pressed,
With drooping tail and humbled crest;
But still the dingle's [2] hollow throat
Prolonged the swelling bugle-note.   175
The owlets started from their dream,
The eagles answered with their scream,
Round and around the sounds were cast,
Till echo seemed an answering blast;
And on the hunter hied his way,   180
To join some comrades of the day;
Yet often paused, so strange the road,
So wondrous were the scenes it showed.

XI

The western waves of ebbing day
Rolled o'er the glen their level way;   185
Each purple peak, each flinty spire,
Was bathed in floods of living fire.
But not a setting beam could glow
Within the dark ravines below,

---

[1] Be to.   [2] Glen.

Where twined the path, in shadow hid,   190
Round many a rocky pyramid,
Shooting abruptly from the dell
Its thunder-splintered pinnacle;
Round many an insulated mass,
The native bulwarks of the pass,   195
Huge as the tower which builders vain
Presumptuous piled on Shinar's plain.
The rocky summits, split and rent,
Formed turret, dome, or battlement,
Or seemed fantastically set   200
With cupola or minaret,
Wild crests as pagod[1] ever decked,
Or mosque of Eastern architect.
Nor were these earth-born castles bare,
Nor lacked they many a banner fair;   205
For, from their shivered brows displayed,
Far o'er the unfathomable glade,
All twinkling with the dewdrop sheen,[2]
The brier-rose fell in streamers green,
And creeping shrubs, of thousand dyes,   210
Waved in the west-wind's summer sighs.

XII

Boon[3] nature scattered, free and wild,
Each plant or flower, the mountain's child.
Here eglantine embalmed the air,
Hawthorn and hazel mingled there;   215

---

[1] Pagoda.   [2] Bright.   [3] Bountiful.

The primrose pale, and violet flower,
Found in each cleft a narrow bower;
Fox-glove and night-shade, side by side,
Emblems of punishment and pride,
Grouped their dark hues with every stain   220
The weather-beaten crags retain.
With boughs that quaked at every breath,
Grey birch and aspen wept beneath;
Aloft, the ash and warrior oak
Cast anchor in the rifted rock;   225
And, higher yet, the pine-tree hung
His shattered trunk, and frequent[1] flung,
Where seemed the cliffs to meet on high,
His boughs athwart the narrowed sky.
Highest of all, where white peaks glanced,   230
Where glistening streamers waved and danced,
The wanderer's eye could barely view
The summer heaven's delicious blue;
So wondrous wild, the whole might seem
The scenery of a fairy dream.   235

XIII

Onward, amid the copse 'gan peep
A narrow inlet, still and deep,
Affording scarce such breadth of brim
As served the wild duck's brood to swim.
Lost for a space, through thickets veering,   240

[1] In abundance.

But broader when again appearing,
Tall rocks and tufted knolls their face
Could on the dark-blue mirror trace;
And farther as the hunter strayed,
Still broader sweep its channels made.   245
The shaggy mounds no longer stood,
Emerging from entangled wood,
But, wave-encircled, seemed to float,
Like castle girdled with its moat;
Yet broader floods extending still   250
Divide them from their parent hill,
Till each, retiring, claims to be
An islet in an inland sea.

XIV

And now, to issue from the glen,
No pathway meets the wanderer's ken,[1]   255
Unless he climb, with footing nice,
A far projecting precipice.
The broom's tough roots his ladder made,
The hazel saplings lent their aid;
And thus an airy point he won,   260
Where, gleaming with the setting sun,
One burnished sheet of living gold,
Loch Katrine lay beneath him rolled;
In all her length far winding lay,
With promontory, creek, and bay,   265

[1] View.

And islands that, empurpled bright,
Floated amid the livelier light,
And mountains that like giants stand
To sentinel enchanted land.
High on the south, huge Benvenue   270
Down to the lake in masses threw
Crags, knolls, and mounds, confusedly hurled,
The fragments of an earlier world;
A wildering [1] forest feathered o'er
His ruined sides and summit hoar,   275
While on the north, through middle air,
Ben-an heaved high his forehead bare.

XV

From the steep promontory gazed
The stranger, raptured and amazed.
And, 'What a scene were here,' he cried,   280
' For princely pomp or churchman's pride !
On this bold brow, a lordly tower;
In that soft vale, a lady's bower;
On yonder meadow, far away,
The turrets of a cloister grey;   285
How blithely might the bugle-horn
Chide on the lake the lingering morn !
How sweet at eve the lover's lute
Chime when the groves were still and mute !
And when the midnight moon should lave   290

[1] Bewildering.

Her forehead in the silver wave,
How solemn on the ear would come
The holy matins' distant hum,
While the deep peal's commanding tone
Should wake, in yonder islet lone,   295
A sainted hermit from his cell,
To drop a bead with every knell!
And bugle, lute, and bell, and all,
Should each bewildered stranger call
To friendly feast and lighted hall.   300

XVI

' Blithe were it then to wander here!
But now — beshrew yon nimble deer —
Like that same hermit's, thin and spare,
The copse must give my evening fare;
Some mossy bank my couch must be,   305
Some rustling oak my canopy.
Yet pass we that; the war and chase
Give little choice of resting-place; —
A summer night in greenwood spent
Were but to-morrow's merriment: 310
But hosts may in these wilds abound,
Such as are better missed than found;
To meet with Highland plunderers here,
Were worse than loss of steed or deer. —
I am alone; — my bugle-strain   315
May call some straggler of the train;

LADY OF THE LAKE — 4

Or, fall the worst that may betide,
Ere now this falchion [1] has been tried.'

XVII

But scarce again his horn he wound,
When lo! forth starting at the sound,   320
From underneath an aged oak
That slanted from the islet rock,
A damsel guider of its way,
A little skiff shot to the bay,
That round the promontory steep   325
Led its deep line in graceful sweep,
Eddying, in almost viewless wave,
The weeping willow twig to lave,
And kiss, with whispering sound and slow,
The beach of pebbles bright as snow.   330
The boat had touched this silver strand,
Just as the hunter left his stand,
And stood concealed amid the brake,
To view this Lady of the Lake.
The maiden paused, as if again   335
She thought to catch the distant strain.
With head upraised, and look intent,
And eye and ear attentive bent,
And locks flung back, and lips apart,
Like monument of Grecian art,   340
In listening mood, she seemed to stand,
The guardian Naiad [2] of the strand.

[1] Short sword.   [2] Water-nymph.

XVIII

And ne'er did Grecian chisel trace
A Nymph, a Naiad, or a Grace,
Of finer form or lovelier face!   345
What though the sun, with ardent frown,
Had slightly tinged her cheek with brown, —
The sportive toil, which, short and light,
Had dyed her glowing hue so bright,
Served too in hastier swell to show   350
Short glimpses of a breast of snow:
What though no rule of courtly grace
To measured mood had trained her pace, —
A foot more light, a step more true,
Ne'er from the heath-flower dashed the dew;   355
E'en the slight harebell raised its head,
Elastic from her airy tread:
What though upon her speech there hung
The accents of the mountain tongue, —
Those silver sounds, so soft, so dear.   360
The listener held his breath to hear!

XIX

A chieftain's daughter seemed the maid;
Her satin snood,[1] her silken plaid,
Her golden brooch, such birth betrayed.
And seldom was a snood amid   365
Such wild luxuriant ringlets hid,

[1] Hair-ribbon.

Whose glossy black to shame might bring
The plumage of the raven's wing;
And seldom o'er a breast so fair,
Mantled a plaid with modest care,   370
And never brooch the folds combined
Above a heart more good and kind.
Her kindness and her worth to spy,
You need but gaze on Ellen's eye;
Not Katrine in her mirror blue   375
Gives back the shaggy banks more true,
Than every free-born glance confessed
The guileless movements of her breast;
Whether joy danced in her dark eye,
Or woe or pity claimed a sigh,   380
Or filial love was glowing there,
Or meek devotion poured a prayer,
Or tale of injury called forth
The indignant spirit of the North.
One only passion unrevealed   385
With maiden pride the maid concealed,
Yet not less purely felt the flame;
O! need I tell that passion's name?

xx

Impatient of the silent horn,
Now on the gale her voice was borne:—   390
'Father!' she cried; the rocks around
Loved to prolong the gentle sound.
A while she paused; no answer came.—

'Malcolm, was thine the blast?' the name
Less resolutely uttered fell ;   395
The echoes could not catch the swell.
'A stranger I,' the huntsman said,
Advancing from the hazel shade.
The maid, alarmed, with hasty oar
Pushed her light shallop[1] from the shore, 400
And when a space was gained between,
Closer she drew her bosom's screen ;
(So forth the startled swan would swing
So turn to prune[2] his ruffled wing.)
Then safe, though fluttered and amazed, 405
She paused, and on the stranger gazed.
Not his the form, nor his the eye,
That youthful maidens wont[3] to fly.

XXI

On his bold visage middle age
Had slightly pressed its signet[4] sage, 410
Yet had not quenched the open truth
And fiery vehemence of youth ;
Forward and frolic glee was there,
The will to do, the soul to dare,
The sparkling glance, soon blown to fire, 415
Of hasty love or headlong ire.
His limbs were cast in manly mould,
For hardy sports or contest bold ;

---

[1] Boat. [2] Arrange. [3] Are accustomed. [4] Seal.

And though in peaceful garb arrayed,
And weaponless, except his blade,   420
His stately mien as well implied
A high-born heart, a martial pride,
As if a baron's crest he wore,
And sheathed in armour trode the shore.
Slighting the petty need he showed,   425
He told of his benighted[1] road;
His ready speech flowed fair and free,
In phrase of gentlest courtesy;
Yet seemed that tone, and gesture bland,
Less used to sue than to command.   430

XXII

A while the maid the stranger eyed,
And, reassured, at length replied,
That Highland halls were open still[2]
To wildered[3] wanderers of the hill.
'Nor think you unexpected come   435
To yon lone isle, our desert home;
Before the heath hath lost the dew,
This morn, a couch was pulled for you;
On yonder mountain's purple head
Have ptarmigan and heath-cock bled,   440
And our broad nets have swept the mere,[4]
To furnish forth your evening cheer.' —
'Now, by the rood,[5] my lovely maid,
Your courtesy has erred,' he said;

[1] Lost.   [2] Always.   [3] Bewildered.   [4] Lake.   [5] Cross.

'No right have I to claim, misplaced,   445
The welcome of expected guest.
A wanderer, here by fortune tost,
My way, my friends, my courser lost,
I ne'er before, believe me, fair,
Have ever drawn your mountain air,   450
Till on this lake's romantic strand,
I found a fay in fairy land!'—

XXIII

'I well believe,' the maid replied,
As her light skiff approached the side,—
'I well believe that ne'er before   455
Your foot has trod Loch Katrine's shore;
But yet, as far as yesternight,
Old Allan-Bane foretold your plight,—
A grey-haired sire, whose eye intent
Was on the visioned future bent.   460
He saw your steed, a dappled grey,
Lie dead beneath the birchen way;
Painted exact your form and mien,
Your hunting-suit of Lincoln green,
That tasselled horn so gaily gilt,   465
That falchion's crooked blade and hilt,
That cap with heron plumage trim,
And yon two hounds so dark and grim.
He bade that all should ready be
To grace a guest of fair degree;   470
But light I held his prophecy,

And deemed it was my father's horn,
Whose echoes o'er the lake were borne.'

XXIV

The stranger smiled:—' Since to your home
A destined errant-knight I come,   475
Announced by prophet sooth[1] and old,
Doomed, doubtless, for achievement bold,
I'll lightly front each high emprise,[2]
For one kind glance of those bright eyes.
Permit me first the task to guide   480
Your fairy frigate o'er the tide.'
The maid, with smile suppressed and sly,
The toil unwonted saw him try;
For seldom sure, if e'er before,
His noble hand had grasped an oar: 485
Yet with main strength his strokes he drew,
And o'er the lake the shallop flew;
With heads erect, and whimpering cry,
The hounds behind their passage ply.
Nor frequent does the bright oar break   490
The dark'ning mirror of the lake,
Until the rocky isle they reach,
And moor their shallop on the beach.

XXV

The stranger viewed the shore around;
'Twas all so close with copsewood bound,   495

[1] True.   [2] Undertaking.

Nor track nor pathway might declare
That human foot frequented there,
Until the mountain maiden showed
A clambering unsuspected road,
That winded through the tangled screen,   500
And opened on a narrow green,
Where weeping birch and willow round
With their long fibres swept the ground.
Here, for retreat in dangerous hour,
Some chief had framed a rustic bower.   505

XXVI

It was a lodge of ample size,
But strange of structure and device;
Of such materials as around
The workman's hand had readiest found.
Lopped of their boughs, their hoar trunks bared, 510
And by the hatchet rudely squared,
To give the walls their destined height
The sturdy oak and ash unite;
While moss and clay and leaves combined
To fence each crevice from the wind.   515
The lighter pine-trees overhead
Their slender length for rafters spread,
And withered heath and rushes dry
Supplied a russet canopy.
Due westward, fronting to the green,   520
A rural portico was seen,

Aloft on native pillars borne
Of mountain fir, with bark unshorn,
Where Ellen's hand had taught to twine
The ivy and Idæan vine,   525
The clematis, the favoured flower
Which boasts the name of virgin-bower,
And every hardy plant could bear
Loch Katrine's keen and searching air.
An instant in this porch she staid,   530
And gaily to the stranger said:
'On heaven and on thy lady call,
And enter the enchanted hall!'

XXVII

'My hope, my heaven, my trust must be,
My gentle guide, in following thee!'   535
He crossed the threshold — and a clang
Of angry steel that instant rang.
To his bold brow his spirit rushed,
But soon for vain alarm he blushed,
When on the floor he saw displayed,   540
Cause of the din, a naked blade
Dropped from the sheath that, careless flung,
Upon a stag's huge antlers swung;
For all around, the walls to grace,
Hung trophies of the fight or chase: 545
A target there, a bugle here,
A battle-ax, a hunting-spear,

And broadswords, bows, and arrows store,[1]
With the tusked trophies of the boar.
Here grins the wolf as when he died,   550
And there the wild-cat's brindled hide
The frontlet of the elk adorns,
Or mantles o'er the bison's horns;
Pennons and flags defaced and stained,
That blackening streaks of blood retained,   555
And deer-skins, dappled, dun, and white,
With otter's fur and seal's unite,
In rude and uncouth tapestry all,
To garnish forth the sylvan hall.

XXVIII

The wandering stranger round him gazed,   560
And next the fallen weapon raised: —
Few were the arms whose sinewy strength
Sufficed to stretch it forth at length:
And as the brand [2] he poised and swayed
'I never knew but one,' he said,   565
'Whose stalwart arm might brook to wield
A blade like this in battle-field.'
She sighed, then smiled and took the word:
'You see the guardian champion's sword;
As light it trembles in his hand   570
As in my grasp a hazel wand;
My sire's tall form might grace the part
Of Ferragus or Ascabart;

[1] In abundance.   [2] Sword.

But in the absent giant's hold [1]
Are women now, and menials [2] old.'   575

XXIX

The mistress of the mansion came,
Mature of age, a graceful dame;
Whose easy step and stately port
Had well become a princely court;
To whom, though more than kindred knew,   580
Young Ellen gave a mother's due.
Meet welcome to her guest she made,
And every courteous rite was paid
That hospitality could claim,
Though all unasked his birth and name.   585
Such then the reverence to a guest,
That fellest [3] foe might join the feast,
And from his deadliest foeman's door
Unquestioned turn, the banquet o'er.
At length his rank the stranger names, —   590
'The Knight of Snowdoun, James Fitz-James;
Lord of a barren heritage,
Which his brave sires, from age to age,
By their good swords had held with toil;
His sire had fallen in such turmoil,   595
And he, God wot, [4] was forced to stand
Oft for his right with blade in hand.
This morning, with Lord Moray's train,

---

[1] Castle.   [2] Servants.   [3] Deadliest.   [4] Knows.

He chased a stalwart *strong* stag in vain,
Outstripped his comrades, missed the deer,   600
Lost his good steed, and wandered here.'

XXX

Now
Fain would the knight in turn require[1]
The name and state of Ellen's sire.
Well showed the elder lady's mien
That courts and cities she had seen;   605
Ellen, though more her looks displayed
The simple grace of sylvan maid,
In speech and gesture, form and face,
Showed she was come of gentle race.
'Twere strange in ruder rank to find   610
Such looks, such manners, and such mind.
Each hint the Knight of Snowdoun gave,
Dame Margaret heard with silence grave;
Or Ellen, innocently gay,
Turned all inquiry light away:—   615
'Weird women[2] we! by dale and down
We dwell, afar from tower and town.
We stem the flood, we ride the blast,
On wandering knights our spells we cast;
While viewless minstrels touch the string,   620
'Tis thus our charméd rhymes we sing.'
She sung, and still[3] a harp unseen
Filled up the symphony between.

[1] Ask.   [2] Witches.   [3] Always.

XXXI

SONG

' Soldier, rest ! thy warfare o'er,
   Sleep the sleep that knows not breaking ;   625
Dream of battled fields no more,
   Days of danger, nights of waking.
In our isle's enchanted hall,
   Hands unseen thy couch are strewing,
Fairy strains of music fall,   630
   Every sense in slumber dewing.
Soldier, rest ! thy warfare o'er,
Dream of fighting fields no more :
Sleep the sleep that knows not breaking,
Morn of toil, nor night of waking.   635

' No rude sound shall reach thine ear,
   Armour's clang, or war-steed champing,
Trump nor pibroch[1] summon here
   Mustering clan or squadron tramping.
Yet the lark's shrill fife may come   640
   At the day-break from the fallow,[2]
And the bittern sound his drum,
   Booming from the sedgy[3] shallow.
Ruder sounds shall none be near,
   Guards nor warders challenge here,   645
Here's no war-steed's neigh and champing,
Shouting clans, or squadron's stamping.'

---

[1] Air played on a bagpipe.   [2] Ploughed land.
   [3] Grassy (overgrown with sedge).

XXXII

She paused — then, blushing, led the lay
To grace the stranger of the day.
Her mellow notes awhile prolong   650
The cadence of the flowing song,
Till to her lips in measured frame
The minstrel verse spontaneous came.

SONG CONTINUED

'Huntsman, rest! thy chase is done;
   While our slumbrous spells assail ye,   655
Dream not, with the rising sun,
   Bugles here shall sound reveillé.[1]
Sleep! the deer is in his den;
   Sleep! thy hounds are by thee lying;
Sleep! nor dream in yonder glen   660
   How thy gallant steed lay dying.
Huntsman, rest! thy chase is done,
Think not of the rising sun,
For at dawning to assail ye
Here no bugles sound reveillé.'   665

XXXIII

The hall was cleared — the stranger's bed
Was there of mountain heather spread,
Where oft a hundred guests had lain,
And dreamed their forest sports again.

[1] Awakening call.

But vainly did the heath-flower shed   670
Its moorland fragrance round his head;
Not Ellen's spell had lulled to rest
The fever of his troubled breast.
In broken dreams the image rose
Of varied perils, pains, and woes: 675
His steed now flounders in the brake,
Now sinks his barge upon the lake;
Now leader of a broken host,
His standard falls, his honour's lost.
Then,—from my couch may heavenly might 680
Chase that worst phantom of the night!—
Again returned the scenes of youth,
Of confident undoubting truth;
Again his soul he interchanged
With friends whose hearts were long estranged.
They come, in dim procession led,   686
The cold, the faithless, and the dead;
As warm each hand, each brow as gay,
As if they parted yesterday.
And doubt distracts him at the view—   690
O were his senses false or true?
Dreamed he of death, or broken vow,
Or is it all a vision now?

XXXIV

At length, with Ellen in a grove
He seemed to walk, and speak of love;   695
She listened with a blush and sigh,

His suit was warm, his hopes were high.
He sought her yielded hand to clasp,
And a cold gauntlet met his grasp:
The phantom's sex was changed and gone,   700
Upon its head a helmet shone;
Slowly enlarged to giant size,
With darkened cheek and threatening eyes,
The grisly[1] visage, stern and hoar,
To Ellen still a likeness bore. —   705
He woke, and, panting with affright,
Recalled the vision of the night.
The hearth's decaying brands[2] were red,
And deep and dusky lustre shed,
Half showing, half concealing, all   710
The uncouth trophies of the hall.
Mid those the stranger fixed his eye,
Where that huge falchion hung on high,
And thoughts on thoughts, a countless throng,
Rushed, chasing countless thoughts along,   715
Until, the giddy whirl to cure,
He rose, and sought the moonshine pure.

XXXV

The wild-rose, eglantine, and broom,
Wasted around their rich perfume;
The birch-trees wept in fragrant balm,   720
The aspens slept beneath the calm;

---

[1] Horrid.   [2] Embers.

The silver light, with quivering glance,
Played on the water's still expanse, —
Wild were the heart whose passion's sway
Could rage beneath the sober ray!   725
He felt its calm, that warrior guest,
While thus he communed with his breast: —
' Why is it, at each turn I trace
Some memory of that exiled race?
Can I not mountain maiden spy,   730
But she must bear the Douglas eye?
Can I not view a Highland brand,
But it must match the Douglas hand?
Can I not frame a fevered dream,
But still the Douglas is the theme?   735
I'll dream no more — by manly mind
Not even in sleep is will resigned.
My midnight orisons[1] said o'er,
I'll turn to rest, and dream no more.'
His midnight orisons he told,   740
A prayer with every bead of gold,
Consigned to heaven his cares and woes,
And sunk in undisturbed repose;
Until the heath-cock shrilly crew,
And morning dawned on Benvenue.   745

[1] Prayers.

CANTO SECOND

The Island

I

At morn the black-cock trims his jetty[1] wing,
  'Tis morning prompts the linnet's blithest lay,
All Nature's children feel the matin spring
  Of life reviving, with reviving day;
And while yon little bark glides down the bay,   5
  Wafting the stranger on his way again,
Morn's genial influence roused a minstrel grey,
  And sweetly o'er the lake was heard thy strain,
Mixed with the sounding harp, O white-haired Allan-
    Bane!

II

SONG

   'Not faster yonder rowers' might   10
      Flings from their oars the spray,
   Not faster yonder rippling bright,
   That tracks the shallop's course in light,
      Melts in the lake away,
   Than men from memory erase   15
   The benefits of former days;
   Then, stranger, go! good speed the while,
   Nor think again of the lonely isle.

[1] Black.

'High place to thee in royal court,
   High place in battled line,   20
Good hawk and hound for sylvan sport!
Where beauty sees the brave resort,
   The honoured meed[1] be thine!
True be thy sword, thy friend sincere,
Thy lady constant, kind, and dear,   25
And lost in love's and friendship's smile
Be memory of the lonely isle.

III

SONG CONTINUED

'But if beneath yon southern sky
   A plaided stranger roam,
Whose drooping crest and stifled sigh,   30
And sunken cheek and heavy eye,
   Pine for his Highland home;
Then, warrior, then be thine to show
The care that soothes a wanderer's woe;
Remember then thy hap erewhile,   35
A stranger in the lonely isle.

'Or if on life's uncertain main
   Mishap shall mar thy sail;
If faithful, wise, and brave in vain,
Woe, want, and exile thou sustain   40
   Beneath the fickle gale;
Waste not a sigh on fortune changed,

---

[1] Reward.

On thankless courts, or friends estranged,
But come where kindred worth shall smile,
To greet thee in the lonely isle.'   45

IV

As died the sounds upon the tide,
The shallop reached the mainland side,
And ere his onward way he took,
The stranger cast a lingering look,
Where easily his eye might reach   50
The harper on the islet beach,
Reclined against a blighted tree,
As wasted, grey, and worn as he.
To minstrel meditation given,
His reverend brow was raised to heaven,   55
As from the rising sun to claim
A sparkle of inspiring flame.
His hand, reclined upon the wire,
Seemed watching the awakening fire;
So still he sate, as those who wait   60
Till judgement speak the doom of fate;
So still, as if no breeze might dare
To lift one lock of hoary hair;
So still, as life itself were fled
In the last sound his harp had sped.   65

V

Upon a rock with lichens wild,
Beside him Ellen sat and smiled. —

Smiled she to see the stately drake
Lead forth his fleet upon the lake,
While her vexed spaniel from the beach   70
Bayed at the prize beyond his reach.
Yet tell me, then, the maid who knows,
Why deepened on her cheek the rose? —
Forgive, forgive, Fidelity !
Perchance the maiden smiled to see   75
Yon parting lingerer wave adieu,
And stop and turn to wave anew;
And, lovely ladies, ere your ire
Condemn the heroine of my lyre,
Show me the fair would scorn to spy   80
And prize such conquest of her eye !

VI

While yet he loitered on the spot,
It seemed as Ellen marked him not;
But when he turned him to the glade,
One courteous parting sign she made;   85
And after, oft the knight would say,
That not, when prize of festal day
Was dealt him by the brightest fair
Who e'er wore jewel in her hair,
So highly did his bosom swell,   90
As at that simple mute farewell.
Now with a trusty mountain-guide,
And his dark stag-hounds by his side,

He parts [1] — the maid, unconscious still,
Watched him wind slowly round the hill;   95
But when his stately form was hid,
The guardian in her bosom chid —
'Thy Malcolm! vain and selfish maid!'
'Twas thus upbraiding conscience said, —
'Not so had Malcolm idly hung   100
On the smooth phrase of southern tongue;
Not so had Malcolm strained his eye,
Another step than thine to spy. —
'Wake, Allan-Bane,' aloud she cried
To the old minstrel by her side, —   105
'Arouse thee from thy moody dream,
I'll give thy harp heroic theme,
And warm thee with a noble name;
Pour forth the glory of the Græme!'
Scarce from her lip the word had rushed,   110
When deep the conscious maiden blushed;
For of his clan, in hall and bower,[2]
Young Malcolm Græme was held the flower.

VII

The minstrel waked his harp — three times
Arose the well-known martial chimes,   115
And thrice their high heroic pride
In melancholy murmurs died.
'Vainly thou bidst, O noble maid,'
Clasping his withered hands, he said,

---

[1] Departs.   [2] Apartment of the women.

'Vainly thou bidst me wake the strain,   120
Though all unwont to bid in vain.
Alas! than mine a mightier hand
Has tuned my harp, my strings has spanned![1]
I touch the chords of joy, but low
And mournful answer notes of woe;   125
And the proud march, which victors tread,
Sinks in the wailing for the dead.
O well for me, if mine alone
That dirge's deep prophetic tone!
If, as my tuneful fathers said,   130
This harp, which erst Saint Modan swayed,
Can thus its master's fate foretell,
Then welcome be the minstrel's knell!

VIII

' But ah! dear lady, thus it sighed
The eve thy sainted mother died;   135
And such the sounds which, while I strove
To wake a lay of war or love,
Came marring all the festal mirth,
Appalling me who gave them birth,
And, disobedient to my call,   140
Wailed loud through Bothwell's bannered hall,
Ere Douglases, to ruin driven,
Were exiled from their native heaven. —
Oh! if yet worse mishap and woe
My master's house must undergo,   145

---

[1] Covered with the hand.

Or aught but weal[1] to Ellen fair
Brood in these accents of despair,
No future bard, sad Harp! shall fling
Triumph or rapture from thy string;
One short, one final strain shall flow,   150
Fraught with unutterable woe,
Then shivered shall thy fragments lie,
Thy master cast him down and die!'

IX

Soothing she answer'd him: ' Assuage,
Mine honoured friend, the fears of age;   155
All melodies to thee are known,
That harp has rung, or pipe has blown,
In Lowland vale or Highland glen,
From Tweed to Spey — what marvel, then,
At times unbidden notes should rise,   160
Confusedly bound in memory's ties,
Entangling, as they rush along,
The war-march with the funeral song? —
Small ground is now for boding fear;
Obscure, but safe, we rest us here.   165
My sire, in native virtue great,
Resigning lordship, lands, and state,
Not then to fortune more resigned
Than yonder oak might give[2] the wind;
The graceful foliage storms may reave,[3]   170
The noble stem they cannot grieve.

[1] Good fortune.   [2] *I.e.*, yield to.   [3] Tear away.

For me,'— she stooped, and, looking round,
Plucked a blue harebell from the ground, —
'For me, whose memory scarce conveys
An image of more splendid days,   175
This little flower, that loves the lea,
May well my simple emblem be;
It drinks heaven's dew as blithe as rose
That in the king's own garden grows;
And when I place it in my hair,   180
Allan, a bard is bound to swear
He ne'er saw coronet so fair.'
Then playfully the chaplet wild
She wreathed in her dark locks, and smiled.

X

Her smile, her speech, with winning sway,   185
Wiled the old harper's mood away.
With such a look as hermits throw,
When angels stoop to soothe their woe,
He gazed, till fond regret and pride
Thrilled to a tear, then thus replied: 190
'Loveliest and best! thou little know'st
The rank, the honours, thou hast lost!
O might I live to see thee grace,
In Scotland's court, thy birth-right place,
To see my favourite's step advance,   195
The lightest in the courtly dance,
The cause of every gallant's sigh,
And leading star of every eye,

And theme of every minstrel's art,
The Lady of the Bleeding Heart!'   200

XI

' Fair dreams are these,' the maiden cried,
(Light was her accent, yet she sighed;)
' Yet is this mossy rock to me
Worth splendid chair and canopy;
Nor would my footstep spring more gay   205
In courtly dance than blithe strathspey,[1]
Nor half so pleased mine ear incline
To royal minstrel's lay as thine.
And then for suitors proud and high,
To bend before my conquering eye, —   210
Thou, flattering bard! thyself wilt say,
That grim Sir Roderick owns its sway.
The Saxon's scourge, Clan-Alpine's pride,
The terror of Loch Lomond's side,
Would, at my suit, thou know'st, delay   215
A Lennox foray[2] — for a day.' —

XII

The ancient bard her glee repressed:
' Ill hast thou chosen theme for jest!
For who, through all this western wild,
Named Black Sir Roderick e'er, and smiled?   220
In Holy-Rood a knight he slew;
I saw, when back the dirk he drew,

---

[1] Highland dance.   [2] Raid.

Courtiers give place before the stride
Of the undaunted homicide ;
And since, though outlawed, hath his hand   225
Full sternly kept his mountain land.
Who else dared give — ah ! woe the day,
That I such hated truth should say —
The Douglas, like a stricken deer,
Disowned by every noble peer,   230
Even the rude refuge we have here ?
Alas ! this wild marauding chief
Alone might hazard our relief,
And, now thy maiden charms expand,
Looks for his guerdon [1] in thy hand ;   235
Full soon may dispensation sought,
To back his suit, from Rome be brought.
Then, though an exile on the hill,
Thy father, as the Douglas, still
Be held in reverence and fear ;   240
And though to Roderick thou'rt so dear,
That thou mightst guide with silken thread,
Slave of thy will, this chieftain dread,
Yet, O loved maid, thy mirth refrain !
Thy hand is on a lion's mane.' —   245

XIII

' Minstrel,' the maid replied, and high
Her father's soul glanced from her eye,

[1] Reward.

'My debts to Roderick's house I know:
All that a mother could bestow,
To Lady Margaret's care I owe,   250
Since first an orphan in the wild
She sorrowed o'er her sister's child;
To her brave chieftain son, from ire
Of Scotland's king who shrouds[1] my sire,
A deeper, holier debt is owed;   255
And, could I pay it with my blood,
Allan! Sir Roderick should command
My blood, my life, — but not my hand.
Rather will Ellen Douglas dwell
A votaress[2] in Maronnan's cell;   260
Rather through realms beyond the sea,
Seeking the world's cold charity,
Where ne'er was spoke a Scottish word,
And ne'er the name of Douglas heard,
An outcast pilgrim will she rove,   265
Than wed the man she cannot love.

XIV

'Thou shak'st, good friend, thy tresses grey, —
That pleading look, what can it say
But what I own? — I grant him brave,
But wild as Bracklinn's thundering wave;   270
And generous — save vindictive mood,
Or jealous transport, chafe his blood:

[1] Protects.   [2] Nun.

I grant him true to friendly band,
As his claymore [1] is to his hand;
But O! that very blade of steel   275
More mercy for a foe would feel:
I grant him liberal, to fling
Among his clan the wealth they bring,
When back by lake and glen they wind,
And in the Lowland leave behind,   280
Where once some pleasant hamlet stood,
A mass of ashes slaked with blood.
The hand that for my father fought
I honour, as his daughter ought;
But can I clasp it reeking red   285
From peasants slaughtered in their shed?
No! wildly while his virtues gleam,
They make his passions darker seem,
And flash along his spirit high,
Like lightning o'er the midnight sky.   290
While yet a child, — and children know,
Instinctive taught, the friend and foe, —
I shuddered at his brow of gloom,
His shadowy plaid, and sable plume;
A maiden grown, I ill could bear   295
His haughty mien and lordly air:
But, if thou join'st a suitor's claim,
In serious mood, to Roderick's name,
I thrill with anguish! or, if e'er
A Douglas knew the word, with fear.   300

---

[1] Large sword.

To change such odious theme were best, —
What thinkst thou of our stranger guest?' —

XV

'What think I of him? — woe the while
That brought such wanderer to our isle!
Thy father's battle-brand, of yore   305
For Tine-man forged by fairy lore,
What time [1] he leagued, no longer foes,
His Border spears with Hotspur's bows,
Did, self-unscabbarded, foreshow
The footstep of a secret foe.   310
If courtly spy hath harboured here,
What may we for the Douglas fear?
What for this island, deemed of old
Clan-Alpine's last and surest hold?
If neither spy nor foe, I pray   315
What yet may jealous Roderick say?
— Nay, wave not thy disdainful head,
Bethink thee of the discord dread
That kindled, when at Beltane game
Thou ledst the dance with Malcolm Græme;   320
Still, though thy sire the peace renewed,
Smoulders in Roderick's breast the feud.
Beware! — But hark, what sounds are these?
My dull ears catch no faltering breeze;
No weeping birch nor aspens wake,   325
Nor breath is dimpling in the lake;

[1] At the time when.

Still is the canna's [1] hoary beard;
Yet, by my minstrel faith, I heard—
And hark again! some pipe of war
Sends the bold pibroch from afar.'   330

XVI

Far up the lengthened lake were spied
Four darkening specks upon the tide,
That, slow enlarging on the view,
Four manned and masted barges grew,
And, bearing downwards from Glengyle,   335
Steered full upon the lonely isle;
The point of Brianchoil they passed,
And, to the windward as they cast,
Against the sun they gave to shine
The bold Sir Roderick's bannered Pine.   340
Nearer and nearer as they bear,
Spears, pikes, and axes flash in air.
Now might you see the tartans [2] brave,
And plaids and plumage dance and wave:
Now see the bonnets sink and rise,   345
As his tough oar the rower plies;
See, flashing at each sturdy stroke,
The wave ascending into smoke;
See the proud pipers on the bow,
And mark the gaudy streamers flow   350
From their loud chanters [3] down, and sweep
The furrowed bosom of the deep,

---

[1] Cotton-grass.   [2] Plaid woollens.   [3] Pipes (of the bagpipe).

As, rushing through the lake amain,
They plied the ancient Highland strain.

XVII

Ever, as on they bore, more loud   355
And louder rung the pibroch proud.
At first the sounds, by distance tame,
Mellowed along the waters came,
And, lingering long by cape and bay,
Wailed every harsher note away;   360
Then, bursting bolder on the ear,
The clan's shrill Gathering[1] they could hear,—
Those thrilling sounds that call the might
Of old Clan-Alpine to the fight.
Thick beat the rapid notes, as when   365
The mustering hundreds shake the glen,
And, hurrying at the signal dread,
The battered earth returns their tread.
Then prelude light, of livelier tone,
Expressed their merry marching on,   370
Ere peal of closing battle rose,
With mingled outcry, shrieks, and blows;
And mimic din of stroke and ward,
As broadsword upon target jarred;
And groaning pause, ere yet again,   375
Condensed, the battle yelled amain;
The rapid charge, the rallying shout,
Retreat borne headlong into rout,

[1] Summons to a gathering.

And bursts of triumph, to declare
Clan-Alpine's conquest — all were there. 580
Nor ended thus the strain; but slow,
Sunk in a moan prolonged and low,
And changed the conquering clarion swell,
For wild lament o'er those that fell.

XVIII

The war-pipes ceased; but lake and hill 385
Were busy with their echoes still;
And, when they slept, a vocal strain
Bade their hoarse chorus wake again,
While loud a hundred clansmen raise
Their voices in their chieftain's praise. 390
Each boatman, bending to his oar,
With measured sweep the burden bore,
In such wild cadence as the breeze
Makes through December's leafless trees.
The chorus first could Allan know, 395
' Roderick Vich Alpine,[1] ho! iro!'
And near, and nearer as they rowed,
Distinct the martial ditty flowed.

XIX

BOAT SONG

' Hail to the chief who in triumph advances!
    Honoured and blessed be the ever-green Pine! 400

[1] Descendant of Alpine.

Long may the tree, in his banner that glances,
  Flourish, the shelter and grace of our line!
      Heaven send it happy dew,
      Earth lend it sap anew,
  Gayly to bourgeon,[1] and broadly to grow,   405
      While every Highland glen
      Sends our shout back again,
  " Roderigh Vich Alpine dhu, ho! ieroe! "

Ours is no sapling, chance-sown by the fountain,
  Blooming at Beltane, in winter to fade;   410
When the whirlwind has stripped every leaf on the
      mountain,
  The more shall Clan-Alpine exult in her shade.
      Moored in the rifted rock,
      Proof to the tempest's shock,
  Firmer he roots him the ruder it blow;   415
      Menteith and Breadalbane, then,
      Echo his praise again,
  " Roderigh Vich Alpine dhu, ho! ieroe! "

XX

SONG CONTINUED

Proudly our pibroch has thrilled in Glen Fruin,
  And Bannochar's groans to our slogan[2] replied; 42c
Glen Luss and Ross-dhu, they are smoking in ruin,
  And the best of Loch Lomond lie dead on her side

---

[1] Bud.   [2] War-cry.

Widow and Saxon maid
Long shall lament our raid,
Think of Clan-Alpine with fear and with woe ; 425
Lennox and Leven-Glen
Shake when they hear again,
" Roderigh Vich Alpine dhu, ho ! ieroe ! "

' Row, vassals, row, for the pride of the Highlands !
Stretch to your oars, for the ever-green Pine ! 430
O that the rose-bud that graces yon islands
Were wreathed in a garland around him to twine !
O that some seedling gem,
Worthy such noble stem,
Honoured and blessed in their shadow might grow !
Loud should Clan-Alpine then 436
Ring from her deepmost glen,
" Roderigh Vich Alpine dhu, ho ! ieroe ! "

XXI

With all her joyful female band,
Had Lady Margaret sought the strand. 440
Loose on the breeze their tresses flew,
And high their snowy arms they threw,
As echoing back with shrill acclaim,
And chorus wild, the chieftain's name ;
While, prompt to please, with mother's art, 445
The darling passion of his heart,
The Dame called Ellen to the strand,
To greet her kinsman ere he land :

'Come, loiterer, come! a Douglas thou,
And shun to wreathe a victor's brow?'   450
Reluctantly and slow, the maid
The unwelcome summoning obeyed,
And, when a distant bugle rung,
In the mid-path aside she sprung:—
'List, Allan-Bane!   From mainland cast,   455
I hear my father's signal blast.
Be ours,' she cried, 'the skiff to guide,
And waft him from the mountain-side.'
Then, like a sunbeam, swift and bright,
She darted to her shallop light,   460
And, eagerly while Roderick scanned,
For her dear form, his mother's band,
The islet far behind her lay,
And she had landed in the bay.

XXII

Some feelings are to mortals given,   465
With less of earth in them than heaven:
And if there be a human tear
From passion's dross refined and clear,
A tear so limpid and so meek,
It would not stain an angel's cheek,   470
'Tis that which pious fathers shed
Upon a duteous daughter's head!
And as the Douglas to his breast
His darling Ellen closely pressed,

Such holy drops her tresses steeped, 475
Though 'twas an hero's eye that weeped.
Nor while on Ellen's faltering tongue
Her filial welcomes crowded hung,
Marked she, that fear (affection's proof)
Still held a graceful youth aloof; 480
No! not till Douglas named his name,
Although the youth was Malcolm Græme.

XXIII

Allan, with wistful look the while,
Marked Roderick landing on the isle;
His master piteously he eyed, 485
Then gazed upon the chieftain's pride,
Then dashed with hasty hand away
From his dimmed eye the gathering spray;
And Douglas, as his hand he laid
On Malcolm's shoulders, kindly said, 490
' Canst thou, young friend, no meaning spy
In my poor follower's glistening eye?
I'll tell thee: — he recalls the day,
When in my praise he led the lay
O'er the arched gate of Bothwell proud, 495
While many a minstrel answered loud,
When Percy's Norman pennon, won
In bloody field, before me shone,
And twice ten knights, the least a name
As mighty as yon chief may claim, 500

Gracing my pomp,[1] behind me came.
Yet trust me, Malcolm, not so proud
Was I of all that marshalled crowd,
Though the waned crescent owned my might,
And in my train trooped lord and knight,   505
Though Blantyre hymned her holiest lays,
And Bothwell's bards flung back my praise,
As when this old man's silent tear,
And this poor maid's affection dear,
A welcome give more kind and true   510
Than aught my better fortunes knew.
Forgive, my friend, a father's boast, —
O, it out-beggars all I lost!'

XXIV

Delightful praise! — Like summer rose,
That brighter in the dew-drop glows,   515
The bashful maiden's cheek appeared,
For Douglas spoke, and Malcolm heard.
The flush of shame-faced joy to hide,
The hounds, the hawk, her cares divide;
The loved caresses of the maid   520
The dogs with crouch and whimper paid;
And, at her whistle, on her hand
The falcon took his favourite stand,
Closed his dark wing, relaxed his eye,
Nor, though unhooded, sought to fly.   525

[1] Procession.

And, trust, while in such guise she stood,
Like fabled goddess of the wood,
That if a father's partial thought
O'erweighed her worth and beauty aught,
Well might the lover's judgement fail　　　530
To balance with a juster scale;
For with each secret glance he stole,
The fond enthusiast sent his soul.

XXV

Of stature fair, and slender frame,
But firmly knit, was Malcolm Græme.　　　535
The belted plaid and tartan hose
Did ne'er more graceful limbs disclose;
His flaxen hair, of sunny hue,
Curled closely round his bonnet blue.
Trained to the chase, his eagle eye　　　540
The ptarmigan in snow could spy:
Each pass, by mountain, lake, and heath,
He knew, through Lennox and Menteith;
Vain was the bound of dark-brown doe,
When Malcolm bent his sounding bow;　　　545
And scarce that doe, though winged with fear,
Outstripped in speed the mountaineer:
Right up Ben-Lomond could he press,
And not a sob his toil confess.
His form accorded with a mind　　　550
Lively and ardent, frank and kind;

A blither heart, till Ellen came,
Did never love nor sorrow tame;
It danced as lightsome in his breast
As played the feather on his crest.   555
Yet friends, who nearest knew the youth,
His scorn of wrong, his zeal for truth,
And bards, who saw his features bold,
When kindled by the tales of old,
Said, were that youth to manhood grown,   560
Not long should Roderick Dhu's renown
Be foremost voiced by mountain fame,
But quail to that of Malcolm Græme.

XXVI

Now back they wend their watery way,
And, ' O my sire!' did Ellen say,   565
' Why urge thy chase so far astray?
And why so late returned? — and why ' —
The rest was in her speaking eye.
' My child, the chase I follow far,
'Tis mimicry of noble war;   570
And with that gallant pastime reft
Were all of Douglas I have left.
I met young Malcolm as I strayed
Far eastward, in Glenfinlas' shade.
Nor strayed I safe; for all around   575
Hunters and horsemen scoured the ground.

¹ Taken away.

This youth, though still a royal ward,
Risked life and land to be my guard,
And through the passes of the wood
Guided my steps, not unpursued;   580
And Roderick shall his welcome make,
Despite old spleen, for Douglas' sake.
Then must he seek Strath-Endrick glen,
Nor peril aught for me again.'

XXVII

Sir Roderick, who to meet them came,   585
Reddened at sight of Malcolm Græme,
Yet not in action, word, or eye,
Failed aught in hospitality.
In talk and sport they whiled away
The morning of that summer day;   590
But at high noon a courier light
Held secret parley with the knight,
Whose moody aspect soon declared,
That evil were the news he heard.
Deep thought seemed toiling in his head;   595
Yet was the evening banquet made,
Ere he assembled round the flame
His mother, Douglas, and the Græme,
And Ellen too; then cast around
His eyes, then fixed them on the ground,   600
As studying phrase that might avail
Best to convey unpleasant tale.

Long with his dagger's hilt he played,
Then raised his haughty brow, and said: —

XXVIII

'Short be my speech; — nor time affords,   605
Nor my plain temper, glozing[1] words.
Kinsman and father, — if such name
Douglas vouchsafe to Roderick's claim;
Mine honoured mother; — Ellen — why,
My cousin, turn away thine eye? —   610
And Græme; in whom I hope to know
Full soon a noble friend or foe,
When age shall give thee thy command
And leading in thy native land, —
List all! — The king's vindictive pride   615
Boasts to have tamed the Border-side,
Where chiefs, with hound and hawk who came
To share their monarch's sylvan game,
Themselves in bloody toils were snared;
And when the banquet they prepared,   620
And wide their loyal portals flung,
O'er their own gateway struggling hung.
Loud cries their blood from Meggat's mead,
From Yarrow braes, and banks of Tweed,
Where the lone streams of Ettrick glide,   625
And from the silver Teviot's side;
The dales, where martial clans did ride,
Are now one sheep-walk, waste and wide.

[1] Smooth, insincere.

This tyrant of the Scottish throne,
So faithless and so ruthless known,   630
Now hither comes; his end the same,
The same pretext of sylvan game.
What grace for Highland chiefs, judge ye
By fate of border chivalry.
Yet more; amid Glenfinlas' green,   635
Douglas, thy stately form was seen —
This by espial[1] sure I know:
Your counsel, in the streight[2] I show?'

XXIX

Ellen and Margaret fearfully
Sought comfort in each other's eye,   640
Then turn'd their ghastly look, each one,
This to her sire — that to her son.
The hasty colour went and came
In the bold cheek of Malcolm Græme;
But from his glance it well appeared   645
'Twas but for Ellen that he feared;
While, sorrowful, but undismay'd,
The Douglas thus his counsel said: —
'Brave Roderick, though the tempest roar,
It may but thunder, and pass o'er;   650
Nor will I here remain an hour,
To draw the lightning on thy bower;
For well thou know'st, at this grey head
The royal bolt were fiercest sped.

[1] The work of spies.   [2] Difficulty.

For thee, who, at thy king's command,   655
Canst aid him with a gallant band,
Submission, homage, humbled pride,
Shall turn the monarch's wrath aside.
Poor remnants of the Bleeding Heart,
Ellen and I will seek, apart,   660
The refuge of some forest cell,
There, like the hunted quarry, dwell,
Till on the mountain and the moor,
The stern pursuit be passed and o'er.'

XXX

'No, by mine honour,' Roderick said,   665
'So help me Heaven, and my good blade!
No, never!   Blasted be yon Pine,
My fathers' ancient crest and mine,
If from its shade in danger part
The lineage of the Bleeding Heart!   670
Hear my blunt speech: grant me this maid
To wife, thy counsel to mine aid;
To Douglas, leagued with Roderick Dhu,
Will friends and allies flock enow[1];
Like cause of doubt, distrust, and grief,   675
Will bind to us each western chief.
When the loud pipes my bridal tell,
The Links of Forth shall hear the knell,
The guards shall start in Stirling's porch;
And, when I light the nuptial torch,   680

[1] Enough.

A thousand villages in flames
Shall scare the slumbers of King James!
— Nay, Ellen, blench [1] not thus away,
And, mother, cease these signs, I pray;
I meant not all my heat might say.   685
Small need of inroad, or of fight,
When the sage Douglas may unite
Each mountain clan in friendly band,
To guard the passes of their land,
Till the foiled king from pathless glen   690
Shall bootless [2] turn him home again.'

XXXI

There are who have, at midnight hour,
In slumber scaled a dizzy tower,
And, on the verge that beetled o'er
The ocean-tide's incessant roar,   695
Dreamed calmly out their dangerous dream,
Till wakened by the morning beam;
When, dazzled by the eastern glow,
Such startler [3] cast his glance below,
And saw unmeasured depth around.   700
And heard unintermitted sound,
And thought the battled fence so frail,
It waved like cobweb in the gale; —
Amid his senses' giddy wheel,
Did he not desperate impulse feel,   705

[1] Shrink.   [2] Without success.   [3] *I.e.* one who is startled.

Headlong to plunge himself below,
And meet the worst his fears foreshow? —
Thus, Ellen, dizzy and astound,[1]
As sudden ruin yawned around,
By crossing terrors wildly tossed,   710
Still for the Douglas fearing most,
Could scarce the desperate thought withstand,
To buy his safety with her hand.

XXXII

Such purpose dread could Malcolm spy
In Ellen's quivering lip and eye,   715
And eager rose to speak — but ere
His tongue could hurry forth his fear,
Had Douglas marked the hectic strife,
Where death seemed combating with life;
For to her cheek, in feverish flood,   720
One instant rushed the throbbing blood,
Then ebbing back, with sudden sway,
Left its domain as wan as clay.
' Roderick, enough ! enough ! ' he cried,
' My daughter cannot be thy bride ;   725
Not that the blush to wooer dear,
Nor paleness that of maiden fear.
It may not be — forgive her, Chief,
Nor hazard aught for our relief.
Against his sovereign, Douglas ne'er   730
Will level a rebellious spear.

[1] Astounded.

'Twas I that taught his youthful hand
To rein a steed and wield a brand;
I see him yet, the princely boy!
Not Ellen more my pride and joy;   735
I love him still, despite my wrongs
By hasty wrath and slanderous tongues.
O seek the grace you well may find,
Without a cause to mine combined!'

XXXIII

Twice through the hall the chieftain strode;   740
The waving of his tartans broad,
And darkened brow, where wounded pride
With ire and disappointment vied,
Seemed, by the torch's gloomy light,
Like the ill demon of the night,   745
Stooping his pinions' shadowy sway
Upon the nighted [1] pilgrim's way:
But, unrequited Love! thy dart
Plunged deepest its envenomed smart,
And Roderick, with thine anguish stung,   750
At length the hand of Douglas wrung,
While eyes that mocked at tears before
With bitter drops were running o'er.
The death-pangs of long-cherished hope
Scarce in that ample breast had scope,   755
But, struggling with his spirit proud,
Convulsive heaved its chequered shroud,[2]

---

[1] Benighted, lost.   [2] Garment.

While every sob — so mute were all —
Was heard distinctly through the hall.
The son's despair, the mother's look,   760
Ill might the gentle Ellen brook ;
She rose, and to her side there came,
To aid her parting steps, the Græme.

XXXIV

Then Roderick from the Douglas broke —
As flashes flame through sable smoke,   765
Kindling its wreaths, long, dark, and low,
To one broad blaze of ruddy glow,
So the deep anguish of despair
Burst, in fierce jealousy, to air.
With stalwart grasp his hand he laid   770
On Malcolm's breast and belted plaid :
' Back, beardless boy ! ' he sternly said,
' Back, minion ! hold'st thou thus at naught
The lesson I so lately taught?
This roof, the Douglas, and that maid,   775
Thank thou for punishment delayed.'
Eager as greyhound on his game,
Fiercely with Roderick grappled Græme.
' Perish my name, if aught afford
Its chieftain safety save his sword ! '   780
Thus as they strove, their desperate hand
Griped to the dagger or the brand,
And death had been — but Douglas rose,

And thrust between the struggling foes
His giant strength : — 'Chieftains, forego !   785
I hold the first who strikes, my foe. —
Madmen, forbear your frantic jar !
What ! is the Douglas fallen so far,
His daughter's hand is deemed the spoil
Of such dishonourable broil ? '   790
Sullen and slowly they unclasp,
As struck with shame, their desperate grasp,
And each upon his rival glared,
With foot advanced, and blade half bared.

XXXV

Ere yet the brands aloft were flung,   795
Margaret on Roderick's mantle hung,
And Malcolm heard his Ellen's scream,
As faltered through terrific dream.
Then Roderick plunged in sheath his sword,
And veiled his wrath in scornful word :   800
' Rest safe till morning ; pity 'twere
Such cheek should feel the midnight air !
Then mayest thou to James Stuart tell,
Roderick will keep the lake and fell,[1]
Nor lackey,[2] with his freeborn clan,   805
The pageant pomp of earthly man.
More would he of Clan-Alpine know,
Thou canst our strength and passes show. —

---

[1] Moor.   [2] Serve as a menial.

Malise, what ho!'—his henchman came;
'Give our safe-conduct to the Græme.' 810
Young Malcolm answered, calm and bold:
'Fear nothing for thy favourite hold;
The spot an angel deigned to grace
Is blessed, though robbers haunt the place.
Thy churlish courtesy for those 815
Reserve, who fear to be thy foes.
As safe to me the mountain way
At midnight as in blaze of day,
Though, with his boldest at his back,
Even Roderick Dhu beset the track.— 820
Brave Douglas,—lovely Ellen,—nay,
Naught of parting will I say.
Earth does not hold a lonesome glen
So secret but we meet again.—
Chieftain! we too shall find an hour.'— 825
He said, and left the sylvan bower.

XXXVI

Old Allan followed to the strand, *shore*
(Such was the Douglas's command,)
And anxious told, how, on the morn,
The stern Sir Roderick deep had sworn, 830
The Fiery Cross should circle o'er
Dale, glen, and valley, down, and moor.
Much were the peril to the Græme,
From those who to the signal came;

Far up the lake 'twere safest land, —   835
Himself would row him to the strand.
He gave his counsel to the wind,
While Malcolm did, unheeding, bind,
Round dirk and pouch and broadsword rolled,
His ample plaid in tightened fold,   840
And stripped his limbs to such array
As best might suit the watery way —

XXXVII

Then spoke abrupt : ' Farewell to thee,
Pattern of old fidelity ! '
The minstrel's hand he kindly pressed, —   845
' O ! could I point [1] a place of rest !
My sovereign holds in ward [2] my land,
My uncle leads my vassal band ;
To tame his foes, his friends to aid,
Poor Malcolm has but heart and blade.   850
Yet, if there be one faithful Græme,
Who loves the chieftain of his name,
Not long shall honoured Douglas dwell,
Like hunted stag, in mountain cell ;
Nor, ere yon pride-swollen robber dare, —   855
I may not give the rest to air !
Tell Roderick Dhu I owed him naught,
Not the poor service of a boat,
To waft me to yon mountain-side.'
Then plunged he in the flashing tide.   860

[1] Show, assign.   [2] Control.

Bold o'er the flood his head he bore,
And stoutly steered him from the shore ;
And Allan strained his anxious eye,
Far 'mid the lake his form to spy,
Darkening across each puny wave,   865
To which the moon her silver gave.
Fast as the cormorant could skim,
The swimmer plied each active limb
Then, landing in the moonlight dell,
Loud shouted, of his weal to tell.   870
The minstrel heard the far halloo,
And joyful from the shore withdrew.

CANTO THIRD

The Gathering

I

Time rolls his ceaseless course.   The race of yore,
  Who danced our infancy upon their knee,
And told our marvelling boyhood legends store [1]
  Of their strange ventures happed by land or sea,
How are they blotted from the things that be!   5
  How few, all weak and withered of their force,
Wait on the verge of dark eternity,
  Like stranded wrecks, the tide returning hoarse,
To sweep them from our sight!   Time rolls his cease-
    less course.

Yet live there still who can remember well,   10
  How, when a mountain chief his bugle blew,
Both field and forest, dingle,[2] cliff, and dell,
  And solitary heath, the signal knew;
And fast the faithful clan around him drew,
  What time the warning note was keenly wound,   15
What time aloft their kindred banner flew,
  While clamorous war-pipes yelled the gathering
    sound,
And while the Fiery Cross glanced, like a meteor, round.

---

[1] In abundance.   [2] Glen.

II

The summer dawn's reflected hue
To purple changed Loch Katrine blue;   20
Mildly and soft the western breeze
Just kissed the lake, just stirred the trees;
And the pleased lake, like maiden coy,
Trembled but dimpled not for joy;
The mountain-shadows on her breast   25
Were neither broken nor at rest;
In bright uncertainty they lie,
Like future joys to Fancy's eye.
The water-lily to the light
Her chalice reared of silver bright;   30
The doe awoke, and to the lawn,
Begemmed with dew-drops, led her fawn;
The grey mist left the mountain-side,
The torrent showed its glistening pride;
Invisible in flecked sky,   35
The lark sent down her revelry;
The blackbird and the speckled thrush
Good-morrow gave from brake and bush;
In answer cooed the cushat dove
Her notes of peace and rest and love.   40

III

No thought of peace, no thought of rest,
Assuaged the storm in Roderick's breast.
With sheathed broadsword in his hand,
Abrupt he paced the islet strand,

And eyed the rising sun, and laid   45
His hand on his impatient blade.
Beneath a rock, his vassals' care
Was prompt the ritual to prepare,
With deep and deathful meaning fraught;
For such Antiquity had taught   50
Was preface meet, ere yet abroad
The Cross of Fire should take its road.
The shrinking band stood oft aghast
At the impatient glance he cast; —
Such glance the mountain-eagle threw,   55
As, from the cliffs of Benvenue,
She spread her dark sails on the wind,
And, high in middle heaven reclined,
With her broad shadow on the lake,
Silenced the warblers of the brake.   60

IV

A heap of withered boughs was piled,
Of juniper and rowan [1] wild,
Mingled with shivers [2] from the oak,
Rent by the lightning's recent stroke.
Brian the Hermit by it stood,   65
Barefooted, in his frock and hood.
His grizzled beard and matted hair
Obscured a visage of despair;
His naked arms and legs, seamed o'er,
The scars of frantic penance bore.   70

[1] Mountain-ash.   [2] Splinters.

That monk, of savage form and face,
The impending danger of his race
Had drawn from deepest solitude,
Far in Benharrow's bosom rude.
Not his the mien of Christian priest,   75
But Druid's, from the grave released,
Whose hardened heart and eye might brook
On human sacrifice to look;
And much, 'twas said, of heathen lore,
Mixed in the charms he muttered o'er.   80
The hallowed creed gave only worse
And deadlier emphasis of curse;
No peasant sought that hermit's prayer,
His cave the pilgrim shunned with care,
The eager huntsman knew his bound,   85
And in mid chase called off his hound;
Or if, in lonely glen or strath,[1]
The desert-dweller met his path,
He prayed, and signed the cross between,
While terror took devotion's mien.   90

v

Of Brian's birth strange tales were told.
His mother watched a midnight fold,
Built deep within a dreary glen,
Where scattered lay the bones of men,
In some forgotten battle slain,   95
And bleached by drifting wind and rain.

[1] Valley.

It might have tamed a warrior's heart
To view such mockery of his art !
The knot-grass fettered there the hand
Which once could burst an iron band ;   100
Beneath the broad and ample bone
That bucklered heart to fear unknown,
A feeble and a timorous guest,
The field-fare framed her lowly nest ;
There the slow blind-worm left his slime   105
On the fleet limbs that mocked at time ;
And there, too, lay the leader's skull,
Still wreathed with chaplet, flushed and full,
For heath-bell with her purple bloom,
Supplied the bonnet and the plume.   110
All night, in this sad glen, the maid
Sat shrouded in her mantle's shade :
— She said no shepherd sought her side,
No hunter's hand her snood untied,
Yet ne'er again, to braid her hair,   115
The virgin snood did Alice wear ;
Nor sought she, from that fatal night,
Or holy church, or blessed rite,   120
But locked her secret in her breast,
And died in travail, unconfessed.

VI

Alone, among his young compeers,[1]
Was Brian from his infant years ;

[1] Associates, equals.

A moody and heart-broken boy,   125
Estranged from sympathy and joy,
Bearing each taunt which careless tongue
On his mysterious lineage flung.
Whole nights he spent by moonlight pale,
To wood and stream his hap to wail,   130
Till, frantic, he as truth received
What of his birth the crowd believed,
And sought, in mist and meteor fire,
To meet and know his phantom sire!
In vain, to soothe his wayward fate,   135
The cloister oped her pitying gate;
In vain the learning of the age
Unclasped the sable-lettered [1] page;
Even in its treasures he could find
Food for the fever of his mind.   140
Eager he read whatever tells
Of magic, cabala, [2] and spells,
And every dark pursuit allied
To curious and presumptuous pride;
Till, with fired brain and nerves o'er-strung, 145
And heart with mystic horrors wrung,
Desperate he sought Benharrow's den,
And hid him from the haunts of men.

VII

The desert gave him visions wild,
Such as might suit the spectre's child.   150

[1] Black-lettered.   [2] Mystical teaching.

Where with black cliffs the torrents toil,
He watched the wheeling eddies boil,
Till, from their foam, his dazzled eyes
Beheld the River Demon rise;
The mountain mist took form and limb   155
Of noontide hag or goblin grim;
The midnight wind came wild and dread,
Swelled with the voices of the dead;
Far on the future battle-heath
His eye beheld the ranks of death: 160
Thus the lone seer, from mankind hurled,
Shaped forth a disembodied world.
One lingering sympathy of mind
Still bound him to the mortal kind;
The only parent he could claim   165
Of ancient Alpine's lineage came.
Late had he heard, in prophet's dream,
The fatal Ben-Shie's boding scream;
Sounds, too, had come in midnight blast,
Of charging steeds, careering fast   170
Along Benharrow's shingly[1] side,
Where mortal horseman ne'er might ride;
The thunderbolt had split the pine, —
All augured ill to Alpine's line.
He girt his loins, and came to show   175
The signals of impending woe,
And now stood prompt to bless or ban,[2]
As bade the chieftain of his clan.

[1] Gravelly.   [2] Curse.

VIII

'Twas all prepared ; — and from the rock
A goat, the patriarch of the flock,   180
Before the kindling pile was laid,
And pierced by Roderick's ready blade.
Patient the sickening victim eyed
The life-blood ebb in crimson tide,
Down his clogged beard and shaggy limb,   185
Till darkness glazed his eyeballs dim.
The grisly priest, with murmuring prayer,
A slender crosslet[1] framed with care,
A cubit's length in measure due ;
The shaft and limbs were rods of yew,   190
Whose parents in Inch-Cailliach wave
Their shadows o'er Clan-Alpine's grave,
And, answering Lomond's breezes deep,
Soothe many a chieftain's endless sleep.
The Cross thus formed he held on high,   195
With wasted hand and haggard eye,
And strange and mingled feelings woke,
While his anathema[2] he spoke.

IX

'Woe to the clansman, who shall view
This symbol of sepulchral yew,   *type of tree*   200
Forgetful that its branches grew

[1] Small cross.   [2] Curse.

Where weep the heavens their holiest dew
   On Alpine's dwelling low!
Deserter of his chieftain's trust,
He ne'er shall mingle with their dust,   205
But, from his sires and kindred thrust,
Each clansman's execration just
   Shall doom him wrath and woe.'
He paused ; — the word the vassals took,
With forward step and fiery look,   210
On high their naked brands they shook,
Their clattering targets wildly strook[1];
   And first in murmur low,
Then, like the billow in his course,
That far to seaward finds his source,   215
And flings to shore his mustered force,
Burst, with loud roar, their answer hoarse,
  'Woe to the traitor, woe!'
Ben-an's grey scalp the accents knew,
The joyous wolf from covert drew,   220
The exulting eagle screamed afar, —
They knew the voice of Alpine's war.

X

The shout was hushed on lake and fell,
The monk resumed his muttered spell:
Dismal and low its accents came,   225
The while he scathed[2] the Cross with flame;

     [1] Struck.   [2] Scarred.

And the few words that reached the air,
Although the holiest name was there,
Had more of blasphemy than prayer.
But when he shook above the crowd   230
Its kindled points, he spoke aloud: —
' Woe to the wretch who fails to rear
At this dread sign the ready spear !
For, as the flames this symbol sear,
His home, the refuge of his fear,   235
    A kindred fate shall know;
Far o'er its roof the volumed flame
Clan-Alpine's vengeance shall proclaim,
While maids and matrons on his name
Shall call down wretchedness and shame,   240
    And infamy and woe.'
Then rose the cry of females, shrill
As goshawk's whistle on the hill,
Denouncing misery and ill,
Mingled with childhood's babbling trill   245
    Of curses stammer'd slow;
Answering, with imprecation dread,
' Sunk be his home in embers red !
And cursed be the meanest shed
That e'er shall hide the houseless head   250
    We doom to want and woe ! '
A sharp and shrieking echo gave,
Coir-Uriskin, thy goblin cave !
And the grey pass where birches wave
    On Beala-nam-bo.   255

XI

Then deeper paused the priest anew,
And hard his labouring breath he drew,
While, with set teeth and clenchèd hand,
And eyes that glowed like fiery brand,
He meditated curse more dread,   260
And deadlier, on the clansman's head,
Who, summoned to his chieftain's aid,
The signal saw and disobeyed.
The crosslet's points of sparkling wood,
He quenched among the bubbling blood,   265
And, as again the sign he reared,
Hollow and hoarse his voice was heard:
'When flits this Cross from man to man,
Vich-Alpine's summons to his clan,
Burst be the ear that fails to heed!   270
Palsied the foot that shuns to speed
May ravens tear the careless eyes,
Wolves make the coward heart their prize!
As sinks that blood-stream in the earth,
So may his heart's-blood drench his hearth! 275
As dies in hissing gore the spark,
Quench thou this light, Destruction dark!
And be the grace to him denied,
Bought by this sign to all beside!'
He ceased; no echo gave again   280
The murmur of the deep Amen.

XII

Then Roderick, with impatient look,
From Brian's hand the symbol took:
'Speed, Malise, speed!' he said, and gave
The crosslet to his henchman brave.   285
'The muster-place be Lanrick mead —
Instant the time — speed, Malise, speed!'
Like heath-bird, when the hawks pursue,
A barge across Loch Katrine flew;
High stood the henchman on the prow;   290
So rapidly the barge-men row,
The bubbles, where they launched the boat,
Were all unbroken and afloat,
Dancing in foam and ripple still,
When it had neared the mainland hill;   295
And from the silver beach's side
Still was the prow three fathom wide,
When lightly bounded to the land
The messenger of blood and brand.

XIII

Speed, Malise, speed! the dun deer's hide   300
On fleeter foot was never tied.
Speed, Malise, speed! such cause of haste
Thine active sinews never braced.
Bend 'gainst the steepy [1] hill thy breast,
Burst down like torrent from its crest;   305

[1] Steep.

With short and springing footstep pass
The trembling bog and false morass;
Across the brook like roebuck bound,
And thread the brake like questing[1] hound:
The crag is high, and scaur[2] is deep,   310
Yet shrink not from the desperate leap:
Parched are thy burning lips and brow,
Yet by the fountain pause not now;
Herald of battle, fate, and fear,
Stretch onward in thy fleet career!   315
The wounded hind thou track'st not now,
Pursuest not maid through greenwood bough,
Nor pliest thou now thy flying pace
With rivals in the mountain race;
But danger, death, and warrior deed   320
Are in thy course — speed, Malise, speed!

XIV

Fast as the fatal symbol flies,
In arms the huts and hamlets rise;
From winding glen, from upland brown,
They poured each hardy tenant down.   325
Nor slacked the messenger his pace;
He showed the sign, he named the place,
And, pressing forward like the wind,
Left clamour and surprise behind.
The fisherman forsook the strand,   330
The swarthy smith took dirk and brand;

---

[1] Seeking the game.   [2] Cliff, precipice.

With changed cheer,[1] the mower blithe
Left in the half-cut swath his scythe;
The herds without a keeper strayed,
The plough was in mid-furrow staid,   335
The falconer tossed his hawk away,
The hunter left the stag at bay;
Prompt at the signal of alarms,
Each son of Alpine rushed to arms;
So swept the tumult and affray   340
Along the margin of Achray.
Alas, thou lovely lake! that e'er
Thy banks should echo sounds of fear!
The rocks, the bosky[2] thickets, sleep
So stilly on thy bosom deep,   345
The lark's blithe carol, from the cloud,
Seems for the scene too gaily loud.

XV

Speed, Malise, speed!—The lake is past,
Duncraggan's huts appear at last,
And peep, like moss-grown rocks, half seen,   350
Half hidden in the copse so green;
There mayest thou rest, thy labour done,
Their lord shall speed the signal on.—
As stoops the hawk upon his prey,
The henchman shot him down the way.   355
—What woeful accents load the gale?
The funeral yell, the female wail!

[1] Look.   [2] Bushy.

A gallant hunter's sport is o'er,
A valiant warrior fights no more.
Who, in the battle or the chase,   360
At Roderick's side shall fill his place —
Within the hall, where torch's ray
Supplies the excluded beams of day,
Lies Duncan on his lowly bier,
And o'er him streams his widow's tear.   365
His stripling son stands mournful by,
His youngest weeps, but knows not why;
The village maids and matrons round
The dismal coronach [1] resound. [2]

XVI

CORONACH

'He is gone on the mountain,   370
    He is lost to the forest,
Like a summer-dried fountain,
    When our need was the sorest.
The font, [3] reappearing,
    From the rain-drops shall borrow,   375
But to us comes no cheering,
    To Duncan no morrow!

'The hand of the reaper
    Takes the ears that are hoary,
But the voice of the weeper   380
    Wails manhood in glory.

[1] Funeral lamentation.   [2] Make to resound.   [3] Fountain, spring.

'The autumn winds rushing
   Waft the leaves that are searest,
But our flower was in flushing,
   When blighting was nearest.   385

'Fleet foot on the correi,[1]
   Sage counsel in cumber,[2]
Red hand in the foray, —
   How sound is thy slumber!
Like the dew on the mountain,   390
   Like the foam on the river,
Like the bubble on the fountain,
   Thou art gone, and for ever!'

XVII

See Stumah, who, the bier beside,
His master's corpse with wonder eyed,   395
Poor Stumah! whom his least halloo
Could send like lightning o'er the dew,
Bristles his crest, and points his ears,
As if some stranger step he hears.
'Tis not a mourner's muffled tread,   400
Who comes to sorrow o'er the dead,
But headlong haste, or deadly fear,
Urge the precipitate career.
All stand aghast: — unheeding all,
The henchman bursts into the hall;   405

---

[1] Hollowed hillside.   [2] Tro'aoie.

Before the dead man's bier he stood;
Held forth the Cross besmeared with blood —
'The muster-place is Lanrick mead —
Speed forth the signal! clansmen, speed!'

XVIII

Angus, the heir of Duncan's line,   410
Sprung forth and seized the fatal sign.
In haste the stripling to his side
His father's dirk and broadsword tied;
But when he saw his mother's eye
Watch him in speechless agony,   415
Back to her opened arms he flew,
Pressed on her lips a fond adieu —
'Alas!' she sobbed, — 'and yet be gone,
And speed thee forth, like Duncan's son!'
One look he cast upon the bier,   420
Dashed from his eye the gathering tear,
Breathed deep to clear his labouring breast,
And tossed aloft his bonnet crest;
Then, like the high-bred colt, when, freed,
First he essays his fire and speed,   425
He vanished, and o'er moor and moss
Sped forward with the Fiery Cross.
Suspended was the widow's tear,
While yet his footsteps she could hear;
And when she marked the henchman's eye   430
Wet with unwonted sympathy,

'Kinsman,' she said, 'his race is run
That should have sped thine errand on;
The oak has fallen, — the sapling bough
Is all Duncraggan's shelter now.   435
Yet trust I well, his duty done,
The orphan's God will guard my son. —
And you, in many a danger true,
At Duncan's hest [1] your blades that drew,
To arms, and guard that orphan's head!   440
Let babes and women wail the dead.'
Then weapon-clang and martial call
Resounded through the funeral hall,
While from the walls the attendant band
Snatched sword and targe [2] with hurried hand;
And short and flitting energy   446
Glanced from the mourner's sunken eye,
As if the sounds to warrior dear
Might rouse her Duncan from his bier.
But faded soon that borrowed force;   450
Grief claimed his right, and tears their course.

XIX

Benledi saw the Cross of Fire,
It glanced like lightning up Strath-Ire.
O'er dale and hill the summons flew,
Nor rest nor pause young Angus knew;   455
The tear that gathered in his eye
He left the mountain breeze to dry;

[1] Command.   [2] Shield.

Until, where Teith's young waters roll
Betwixt him and a wooded knoll
That graced the sable strath [1] with green,   460
The chapel of St. Bride was seen.
Swoln was the stream, remote the bridge,
But Angus paused not on the edge;
Though the dark waves danced dizzily,
Though reeled his sympathetic eye,   465
He dashed amid the torrent's roar:
His right hand high the crosslet bore,
His left the pole-ax grasped, to guide
And stay his footing in the tide.
He stumbled twice — the foam splashed high,
With hoarser swell the stream raced by;   471
And had he fallen, — for ever there,
Farewell Duncraggan's orphan heir!
But still, as if in parting life,
Firmer he grasped the Cross of strife,   475
Until the opposing bank he gained,
And up the chapel pathway strained.

XX

A blithesome rout,[2] that morning tide,[3]
Had sought the chapel of St. Bride.
Her troth Tombea's Mary gave
To Norman, heir of Armandave,   480
And, issuing from the Gothic arch,
The bridal now resumed their march.

[1] Dark valley.   [2] Company.   [3] Time.

In rude but glad procession came
Bonneted sire and coif-clad dame;   485
And plaided youth, with jest and jeer,
Which snooded maiden would not hear;
And children, that, unwitting[1] why,
Lent the gay shout their shrilly cry;
And minstrels, that in measures vied   490
Before the young and bonny bride,
Whose downcast eye and cheek disclose
The tear and blush of morning rose.
With virgin step, and bashful hand,
She held the kerchief's snowy band;   495
The gallant bridegroom by her side
Beheld his prize with victor's pride,
And the glad mother in her ear
Was closely whispering word of cheer.

XXI

Who meets them at the churchyard gate?   500
The messenger of fear and fate!
Haste in his hurried accent lies,
And grief is swimming in his eyes.
All dripping from the recent flood,
Panting and travel-soiled he stood,   505
The fatal sign of fire and sword
Held forth, and spoke the appointed word:
'The muster-place is Lanrick mead —
Speed forth the signal! Norman, speed!'

[1] Not knowing.

And must he change so soon the hand,   515
Just linked to his by holy band,
For the fell Cross of blood and brand?
And must the day so blithe that rose,
And promised rapture in the close,
Before its setting hour, divide   515
The bridegroom from the plighted bride?
O fatal doom! — it must! it must!
Clan-Alpine's cause, her chieftain's trust,
Her summons dread, brook no delay;
Stretch to the race — away! away!   520

XXII

Yet slow he laid his plaid aside,
And, lingering, eyed his lovely bride,
Until he saw the starting tear
Speak woe he might not stop to cheer;
Then, trusting not a second look,   525
In haste he sped him up the brook,
Nor backward glanced, till on the heath
Where Lubnaig's lake supplies the Teith.
— What in the racer's bosom stirred?
The sickening pang of hope deferred,   530
And memory, with a torturing train
Of all his morning visions vain.
Mingled with love's impatience, came
The manly thirst for martial fame,
The stormy joy of mountaineers,   535
Ere yet they rush upon the spears,

And zeal for clan and chieftain burning,
And hope, from well-fought field returning,
With war's red honours on his crest,
To clasp his Mary to his breast.   540
Stung by such thoughts, o'er bank and brae,[1]
Like fire from flint he glanced away,
While high resolve and feeling strong
Burst into voluntary song.

XXIII

SONG

'The heath this night must be my bed,   545
  The bracken[2] curtain for my head,
My lullaby the warder's tread,
    Far, far, from love and thee, Mary;
To-morrow eve, more stilly laid,
My couch may be my bloody plaid,   550
My vesper song thy wail, sweet maid!
    It will not waken me, Mary!

'I may not, dare not, fancy now
  The grief that clouds thy lovely brow;
I dare not think upon thy vow,   555
    And all it promised me, Mary!
No fond regret must Norman know;
When bursts Clan-Alpine on the foe,
His heart must be like bended bow,
    His foot like arrow free, Mary.   560

          [1] Hillside.   [2] Fern.

'A time will come with feeling fraught,
For, if I fall in battle fought,
Thy hapless lover's dying thought
   Shall be a thought of thee, Mary.
And if returned from conquered foes,   565
How blithely will the evening close,
How sweet the linnet sing repose,
   To my young bride and me, Mary!'

XXIV

Not faster o'er thy heathery braes,
Balquidder, speeds the midnight blaze,   570
Rushing, in conflagration strong,
Thy deep ravines and dells along,
Wrapping thy cliffs in purple glow,
And reddening the dark lakes below;
Nor faster speeds it, nor so far,   575
As o'er thy heaths the voice of war.
The signal roused to martial coil[1]
The sullen margin of Loch Voil,
Waked still Loch Doine, and to the source
Alarmed, Balvaig, thy swampy course;   580
Thence southward turned its rapid road
Adown Strath-Gartney's valley broad,
Till rose in arms each man might claim
A portion in Clan-Alpine's name,
From the grey sire, whose trembling hand   585
Could hardly buckle on his brand,

[1] Tumult.

To the raw boy, whose shaft and bow
Were yet scarce terror to the crow.
Each valley, each sequestered glen,
Mustered its little horde of men,   390
That met as torrents from the height
In Highland dales their streams unite,
Still gathering, as they pour along,
A voice more loud, a tide more strong,
Till at the rendezvous they stood   595
By hundreds, prompt for blows and blood;
Each trained to arms since life began,
Owning no tie but to his clan,
No oath but by his chieftain's hand,
No law but Roderick Dhu's command.   600

XXV

That summer morn had Roderick Dhu
Surveyed the skirts of Benvenue,
And sent his scouts o'er hill and heath,
To view the frontiers of Menteith.
All backward came with news of truce;   605
Still lay each martial Græme and Bruce;
In Rednoch courts no horsemen wait,
No banner waved on Cardross gate,
On Duchray's towers no beacon shone,
Nor scared the herons from Loch Con;   610
All seemed at peace. — Now wot[1] ye why
The chieftain, with such anxious eye,

[1] Know.

Ere to the muster he repair,
This western frontier scanned with care? —
In Benvenue's most darksome cleft,   615
A fair, though cruel, pledge was left;
For Douglas, to his promise true,
That morning from the isle withdrew,
And in a deep sequestered dell
Had sought a low and lonely cell.   620
By many a bard, in Celtic tongue,
Has Coir-nan-Uriskin been sung;
A softer name the Saxons gave,
And called the grot the Goblin Cave.

XXVI

It was a wild and strange retreat,   625
As e'er was trod by outlaw's feet.
The dell, upon the mountain's crest,
Yawned like a gash on warrior's breast;
Its trench had staid full many a rock,
Hurled by primeval earthquake shock   630
From Benvenue's grey summit wild,
And here, in random ruin piled,
They frowned incumbent o'er the spot,
And formed the rugged sylvan grot.
The oak and birch, with mingled shade,   635
At noontide there a twilight made,
Unless when short and sudden shone
Some straggling beam on cliff or stone,
With such a glimpse as prophet's eye

Gains on thy depth, Futurity. 640
No murmur waked the solemn still,[1]
Save tinkling of a fountain rill;
But when the wind chafed with the lake,
A sullen sound would upward break,
With dashing hollow voice, that spoke 645
The incessant war of wave and rock.
Suspended cliffs, with hideous sway,
Seemed nodding o'er the cavern grey.
From such a den the wolf had sprung,
In such the wild-cat leaves her young; 650
Yet Douglas and his daughter fair
Sought for a space their safety there.
Grey Superstition's whisper dread
Debarred the spot to vulgar tread;
For there, she said, did fays[2] resort, 655
And satyrs[3] hold their sylvan court,
By moonlight tread their mystic maze,
And blast the rash beholder's gaze.

XXVII

Now eve, with western shadows long,
Floated on Katrine bright and strong, 660
When Roderick, with a chosen few,
Repassed the heights of Benvenue.
Above the Goblin Cave they go,
Through the wild pass of Beal-nam-bo;

[1] Stillness.　　　[2] Fairies.　　　[3] Fabled creatures of the woods.

The prompt retainers speed before,   565
To launch the shallop from the shore,
For 'cross Loch Katrine lies his way
To view the passes of Achray,
And place his clansmen in array.
Yet lags the chief in musing mind,   670
Unwonted sight, his men behind.
A single page, to bear his sword,
Alone attended on his lord;
The rest their way through thickets break,
And soon await him by the lake.   675
It was a fair and gallant sight,
To view them from the neighbouring height,
By the low-levelled sunbeams light!
For strength and stature, from the clan
Each warrior was a chosen man,   680
As even afar might well be seen,
By their proud step and martial mien.
Their feathers dance, their tartans float,
Their targets gleam, as by the boat
A wild and warlike group they stand,   685
That well became such mountain-strand.

XXVIII

Their chief, with step reluctant, still
Was lingering on the craggy hill,
Hard by where turned apart the road
To Douglas's obscure abode.   690
It was but with that dawning morn

That Roderick Dhu had proudly sworn
To drown his love in war's wild roar,
Nor think of Ellen Douglas more;
But he who stems a stream with sand,   695
And fetters flame with flaxen band,
Has yet a harder task to prove —
By firm resolves to conquer love!
Eve finds the chief, like restless ghost,
Still hovering near his treasure lost;   700
For though his haughty heart deny
A parting meeting to his eye,
Still fondly strains his anxious ear
The accents of her voice to hear,
And inly did he curse the breeze   705
That waked to sound the rustling trees.
But hark! what mingles in the strain?
It is the harp of Allan-Bane,
That wakes its measure slow and high,
Attuned to sacred minstrelsy.   710
What melting voice attends the strings?
'Tis Ellen, or an angel, sings.

XXIX

HYMN TO THE VIRGIN

'*Ave Maria!*'[1] maiden mild!
    Listen to a maiden's prayer!
Thou canst hear though from the wild,   715
    Thou canst save amid despair.

[1] Hail Mary.

'Safe may we sleep beneath thy care,
    Though banished, outcast, and reviled —
Maiden! hear a maiden's prayer!
    Mother, hear a suppliant child!   720
                    Ave Maria!

'*Ave Maria!* undefiled!
    The flinty couch we now must share
Shall seem with down of eider piled,
    If thy protection hover there.
The murky cavern's heavy air   725
    Shall breathe of balm if thou hast smiled;
Then, Maiden! hear a maiden's prayer!
    Mother, list a suppliant child!
                    Ave Maria!

'*Ave Maria!* stainless styled!
    Foul demons of the earth and air,   730
From this their wonted haunt exiled,
    Shall flee before thy presence fair.
We bow us to our lot of care,
    Beneath thy guidance reconciled;
Hear for a maid a maiden's prayer!   735
    And for a father hear a child!
                    Ave Maria!'

XXX

Died on the harp the closing hymn. —
Unmoved in attitude and limb,

As listening still, Clan-Alpine's lord
Stood leaning on his heavy sword, 740
Until the page, with humble sign,
Twice pointed to the sun's decline.
Then, while his plaid he round him cast,
' It is the last time — 'tis the last,'
He muttered thrice, — ' the last time e'er 745
That angel voice shall Roderick hear ! '
It was a goading thought — his stride
Hied hastier [1] down the mountain-side ;
Sullen he flung him in the boat,
And instant [2] 'cross the lake it shot. 750
They landed in that silvery bay,
And eastward held their hasty way,
Till, with the latest beams of light,
The band arrived on Lanrick height,
Where mustered, in the vale below, 755
Clan-Alpine's men in martial show.

XXXI

A various scene the clansmen made ;
Some sat, some stood, some slowly strayed ;
But most, with mantles folded round,
Were couched to rest upon the ground, 760
Scarce to be known by curious eye
From the deep heather where they lie,
So well was matched the tartan screen
With heath-bell dark and brackens green ;

---

[1] Hastened more rapidly.   [2] Instantly.

Unless where, here and there, a blade　　765
Or lance's point a glimmer made,
Like glow-worm twinkling through the shade.
But when, advancing through the gloom,
They saw the chieftain's eagle plume,
Their shout of welcome, shrill and wide,　　770
Shook the steep mountain's steady side.
Thrice it arose, and lake and fell
Three times returned the martial yell;
It died upon Bochastle's plain,
And Silence claimed her evening reign.　　775

CANTO FOURTH

THE PROPHECY

I

'The rose is fairest when 'tis budding new,
  And hope is brightest when it dawns from fears;
The rose is sweetest washed with morning dew,
  And love is loveliest when embalmed in tears.
O wilding[1] rose, whom fancy thus endears,   5
  I bid your blossoms in my bonnet wave,
Emblem of hope and love through future years!' —
  Thus spoke young Norman, heir of Armandave,
What time the sun arose on Vennachar's broad wave.

II

Such fond conceit, half said, half sung,   10
Love prompted to the bridegroom's tongue.
All while he stripped the wild-rose spray,
His ax and bow beside him lay,
For on a pass 'twixt lake and wood,
A wakeful sentinel he stood.   15
Hark! on the rock a footstep rung,
And instant to his arms he sprung.
'Stand, or thou diest! — What, Malise? — soon
Art thou returned from Braes of Doune.

[1] Wild.

By thy keen step and glance I know   20
Thou bring'st us tidings of the foe.'—
(For while the Fiery Cross hied on,
On distant scout[1] had Malise gone.)
'Where sleeps the chief?' the henchman said.—
'Apart, in yonder misty glade;   25
To his lone couch I'll be your guide.'—
Then called a slumberer by his side,
And stirred him with his slackened bow—
'Up, up, Glentarkin! rouse thee, ho!
We seek the chieftain; on the track   30
Keep eagle watch till I come back.'

III

Together up the pass they sped:
'What of the foemen?' Norman said.—
'Varying reports from near and far;
This certain,— that a band of war   35
Has for two days been ready boune,[2]
At prompt command, to march from Doune;
King James, the while, with princely powers,
Holds revelry in Stirling towers.
Soon will this dark and gathering cloud   40
Speak on our glens in thunder loud.
Inured[3] to bide[4] such bitter bout,[5]
The warrior's plaid may bear it out;

---

[1] Scouting expedition.   [2] Prepared.   [3] Trained.   [4] Endure.
[5] Trial of strength.

But, Norman, how wilt thou provide
A shelter for thy bonny bride?'—   45
'What! know ye not that Roderick's care
To the lone isle hath caused repair
Each maid and matron of the clan,
And every child and aged man
Unfit for arms; and given his charge,   50
Nor skiff nor shallop, boat nor barge,
Upon these lakes shall float at large,
But all beside the islet moor,
That such dear pledge may rest secure?'—

IV

' 'Tis well advised[1]—the chieftain's plan   55
Bespeaks the father of his clan.
But wherefore sleeps Sir Roderick Dhu
Apart from all his followers true?'—
'It is because last evening-tide
Brian an augury hath tried,   60
Of that dread kind which must not be
Unless in dread extremity,—
The Taghairm called; by which, afar,
Our sires foresaw the events of war.
Duncraggan's milk-white bull they slew.'—   65

MALISE

'Ah! well the gallant brute I knew!
The choicest of the prey we had,

[1] Planned.

When swept our merry-men Gallangad.
His hide was snow, his horns were dark,
His red eye glowed like fiery spark;   70
So fierce, so tameless, and so fleet,
Sore did he cumber our retreat,
And kept our stoutest kerns[1] in awe,
Even at the pass of Beal 'maha.
But steep and flinty was the road,   75
And sharp the hurrying pikemen's goad,
And when we came to Dennan's Row
A child might scathless[2] stroke his brow.'

V

NORMAN

'That bull was slain: his reeking hide
They stretched the cataract beside,   80
Whose waters their wild tumult toss
Adown the black and craggy boss[3]
Of that huge cliff whose ample verge[4]
Tradition calls the Hero's Targe.
Couched on a shelf beneath its brink,   85
Close where the thundering torrents sink,
Rocking beneath their headlong sway,
And drizzled by the ceaseless spray,
Midst groan of rock and roar of stream,
The wizard waits prophetic dream.   90
Nor distant rests the chief; — but hush!

[1] Light-armed soldiers.   [2] Without harm.   [3] Knob.
[4] Broad edge.

See, gliding slow through mist and bush,
The hermit gains yon rock, and stands
To gaze upon our slumbering bands.
Seems he not, Malise, like a ghost,   95
That hovers o'er a slaughtered host?
Or raven on the blasted oak,
That, watching while the deer is broke,[1]
His morsel claims with sullen croak?'

MALISE

'Peace! peace! to other than to me,   100
Thy words were evil augury;
But still I hold Sir Roderick's blade
Clan-Alpine's omen and her aid,
Not aught that, gleaned from heaven or hell,
Yon fiend-begotten monk can tell.   105
The chieftain joins him, see — and now
Together they descend the brow.'

VI

And, as they came, with Alpine's lord
The hermit monk held solemn word : —
'Roderick! it is a fearful strife,   110
For man endowed with mortal life,
Whose shroud of sentient clay can still
Feel feverish pang and fainting chill,
Whose eye can stare in stony trance,
Whose hair can rouse[2] like warrior's lance, — 115

[1] Quartered.   [2] Rise.

'Tis hard for such to view, unfurled,
The curtain of the future world.
Yet, witness every quaking limb,
My sunken pulse, mine eyeballs dim,
My soul with harrowing anguish torn,   120
This for my chieftain have I borne! —
The shapes that sought my fearful couch
A human tongue may ne'er avouch;[1]
No mortal man — save he who, bred
Between the living and the dead,   125
Is gifted beyond nature's law —
Had e'er survived to say he saw.
At length the fateful answer came,
In characters of living flame!
Not spoke in word, nor blazed in scroll,   130
But borne and branded on my soul: —
WHICH SPILLS THE FOREMOST FOEMAN'S LIFE,
THAT PARTY CONQUERS IN THE STRIFE.' —

VII

'Thanks, Brian, for thy zeal and care!
Good is thine augury,[2] and fair.   135
Clan-Alpine ne'er in battle stood
But first our broadswords tasted blood.
A surer victim still I know,
Self-offered to the auspicious blow:
A spy has sought my land this morn, —   140
No eve shall witness his return!

[1] Confess.   [2] Prophecy.

My followers guard each pass's mouth,
To east, to westward, and to south,
Red Murdoch, bribed to be his guide,
Has charge to lead his steps aside, 145
Till, in deep path or dingle brown,
He light on those shall bring him down.
— But see who comes his news to show!
Malise! what tidings of the foe?'—

VIII

'At Doune, o'er many a spear and glaive[1] 150
Two barons proud their banners wave.
I saw the Moray's silver star,
And marked the sable pale[2] of Mar.'—
'By Alpine's soul, high tidings those!
I love to hear of worthy foes. 155
When move they on?'—'To-morrow's noon
Will see them here for battle boune.'—
'Then shall it see a meeting stern!—
But, for the place — say, couldst thou learn
Nought of the friendly clans of Earn? 160
Strengthened by them, we well might bide
The battle on Benledi's side.
Thou couldst not?— well! Clan-Alpine's men
Shall man the Trosachs' shaggy glen;
Within Loch Katrine's gorge we'll fight, 165
All in our maids' and matrons' sight,

---

[1] Broadsword.   [2] Black stripe in a coat-of-arms.

Each for his hearth and household fire,
Father for child, and son for sire,
Lover for maid beloved ! — But why —
Is it the breeze affects mine eye?   170
Or dost thou come, ill-omened tear !
A messenger of doubt or fear?
No ! sooner may the Saxon lance
Unfix Benledi from his stance,[1]
Than doubt or terror can pierce through   175
The unyielding heart of Roderick Dhu !
'Tis stubborn as his trusty targe.
Each to his post ! — all know their charge.'
The pibroch sounds, the bands advance,
The broadswords gleam, the banners dance,   180
Obedient to the chieftain's glance.
— I turn me from the martial roar,
And seek Coir-Uriskin once more.

IX

Where is the Douglas ? — he is gone;
And Ellen sits on the grey stone   185
Fast by the cave, and makes her moan ;
While vainly Allan's words of cheer
Are poured on her unheeding ear. —
He will return — dear lady, trust ! —
With joy return ; — he will — he must.   190
Well was it time to seek afar
Some refuge from impending war,

[1] Station.

When e'en Clan-Alpine's rugged swarm
Are cowed by the approaching storm.
I saw their boats, with many a light,   195
Floating the livelong yesternight,
Shifting like flashes darted forth
By the red streamers of the north;
I marked at morn how close they ride,
Thick moored by the lone islet's side,   200
Like wild ducks couching in the fen,
When stoops the hawk upon the glen.
Since this rude race dare not abide
The peril on the mainland side,
Shall not thy noble father's care   205
Some safe retreat for thee prepare?'—

X

ELLEN

'No, Allan, no!   Pretext so kind
My wakeful terrors could not blind.
When in such tender tone, yet grave,
Douglas a parting blessing gave,   210
The tear that glistened in his eye
Drowned not his purpose fixed and high.
My soul, though feminine and weak,
Can image his; e'en as the lake,
Itself disturbed by slightest stroke,   215
Reflects the invulnerable rock.
He hears report of battle rife,
He deems himself the cause of strife.

I saw him redden when the theme
Turned, Allan, on thine idle dream   220
Of Malcolm Græme in fetters bound,
Which I, thou saidst, about him wound.
Think'st thou he trowed[1] thine omen aught?
Oh no! 'twas apprehensive thought
For the kind youth, — for Roderick too —   225
(Let me be just) that friend so true;
In danger both, and in our cause!
Minstrel, the Douglas dare not pause.
Why else that solemn warning given, —
"If not on earth, we meet in heaven"?   230
Why else, to Cambus-Kenneth's fane,[2]
If eve return him not again,
Am I to hie, and make me known?
Alas! he goes to Scotland's throne,
Buys his friends' safety with his own;   235
He goes to do — what I had done,
Had Douglas' daughter been his son!' —

XI

'Nay, lovely Ellen! — dearest, nay!
If aught should his return delay,
He only named yon holy fane   240
As fitting place to meet again.
Be sure he's safe; and for the Græme, —
Heaven's blessing on his gallant name! —
My visioned sight may yet prove true,

[1] Believed.   [2] Shrine, church.

Nor bode of ill to him or you. 245
When did my gifted dream beguile?
Think of the stranger at the isle,
And think upon the harpings slow
That presaged this approaching woe!
Sooth[1] was my prophecy of fear; 250
Believe it when it augurs[2] cheer.
Would we had left this dismal spot!
Ill luck still haunts a fairy grot.
Of such a wondrous tale I know —
Dear lady, change that look of woe; 255
My harp was wont thy grief to cheer.' —

ELLEN

'Well, be it as thou wilt; I hear,
But cannot stop the bursting tear.'
The minstrel tried his simple art,
But distant far was Ellen's heart. 260

XII

BALLAD

Alice Brand

'Merry it is in the good greenwood,
  When the mavis[3] and merle[4] are singing,
When the deer sweeps by, and the hounds are in cry,
  And the hunter's horn is ringing.

True.   [2] Predicts.   [3] Thrush.   [4] Blackbird.

' " O Alice Brand, my native land   265
    Is lost for love of you;
And we must hold by wood and wold,[1]
    As outlaws wont to do.

' " O Alice, 'twas all for thy locks so bright,
    And 'twas all for thine eyes so blue,   270
'That on the night of our luckless flight,
    Thy brother bold I slew.

' " Now must I teach to hew the beech
    The hand that held the glaive,
For leaves to spread our lowly bed,   275
    And stakes to fence our cave.

' " And for vest of pall,[2] thy fingers small,
    That wont[3] on harp to stray,
A cloak must shear from the slaughtered deer,
    To keep the cold away." —   280

' " O Richard! if my brother died,
    'Twas but a fatal chance;
For darkling[4] was the battle tried,
    And fortune sped the lance.

' " If pall and vair[5] no more I wear,   285
    Nor thou the crimson sheen,[6]
As warm, we'll say, is the russet grey,
    As gay the forest-green.

' Open country.   2 Fine cloth.   3 Are accustomed.
    4 In the dark.   5 Squirrel-fur.   6 Shining.

" And, Richard, if our lot be hard,
    And lost thy native land,
Still Alice has her own Richard,
    And he his Alice Brand." 290

XIII

BALLAD CONTINUED

'Tis merry, 'tis merry, in good greenwood,
    So blithe Lady Alice is singing ;
On the beech's pride, and oak's brown side, 295
    Lord Richard's ax is ringing.

' Up spoke the moody elfin king,
    Who woned [1] within the hill, —
Like wind in the porch of a ruined church,
    His voice was ghostly shrill. 300

" Why sounds yon stroke on beech and oak,
    Our moonlight circle's screen ?
Or who comes here to chase the deer,
    Beloved of our elfin queen ?
Or who may dare on wold to wear 305
    The fairies' fatal green !

' " Up, Urgan, up ! to yon mortal hie,
    For thou wert christened man ;
For cross or sign thou wilt not fly,
    For muttered word or ban. [2] 310

[1] Dwelt.   [2] Curse.

' " Lay on him the curse of the withered heart,
    The curse of the sleepless eye ;
Till he wish and pray that his life would part,
    Nor yet find leave to die."

XIV

BALLAD CONTINUED

' 'Tis merry, 'tis merry, in good greenwood,   315
    Though the birds have stilled their singing ;
The evening blaze doth Alice raise,
    And Richard is fagots bringing.

' Up Urgan starts, that hideous dwarf,
    Before Lord Richard stands,   320
And, as he crossed and blessed himself,
    " I fear not sign," quoth the grisly [1] elf,
    " That is made with bloody hands."

' But out then spoke she, Alice Brand,
    That woman void of fear, —   325
" And if there's blood upon his hand,
    'Tis but the blood of deer." —

' " Now loud thou liest, thou bold of mood !
    It cleaves unto his hand,
The stain of thine own kindly [2] blood,   330
    The blood of Ethert Brand."

[1] Horrid.   [2] Natural, kindred.

' Then forward stepped she, Alice Brand,
  And made the holy sign, —
 " And if there's blood on Richard's hand,
  A spotless hand is mine.   335

 " And I conjure thee, demon elf,
  By Him whom demons fear,
To show us whence thou art thyself,
  And what thine errand here? "

XV

BALLAD CONTINUED

' " 'Tis merry, 'tis merry, in Fairy-land, 340
  When fairy birds are singing,
When the court doth ride by their monarch's side,
  With bit and bridle ringing :

' " And gaily shines the Fairy-land —
  But all is glistening show,   345
Like the idle gleam that December's beam
  Can dart on ice and snow.

' " And fading, like that varied gleam,
  Is our inconstant shape,
Who now like knight and lady seem, 350
  And now like dwarf and ape.

' " It was between the night and day,
  When the fairy king has power,

That I sunk down in a sinful fray,
And 'twixt life and death was snatched **away**   355
   To the joyless elfin bower.

⁵ " But wist I ¹ of a woman bold,
   Who thrice my brow durst sign,²
I might regain my mortal mould,³
   As fair a form as thine."   360

⁶ She crossed him once — she crossed him twice —
   That lady was so brave ;
The fouler grew his goblin hue,
   The darker grew the cave.

¹ She crossed him thrice, that lady **bold** ;   365
   He rose beneath her hand
The fairest knight on Scottish **mould**,⁴
   Her brother, Ethert Brand !

⁸ Merry it is in good greenwood,
   When the mavis and merle are singing,   370
But merrier were they in Dunfermline **grey**,
   When all the bells were ringing.'

XVI

Just as the minstrel sounds were stai**d**,
A stranger climbed the steepy glade ;
His martial step, his stately mien,   375
His hunting-suit of Lincoln green,

---

¹ If I knew.   ² Mark with the sign of the cross.   ⁸ Shape.
⁴ Ground.

His eagle glance, remembrance claims —
'Tis Snowdoun's knight, 'tis James Fitz-James.
Ellen beheld as in a dream,
Then, starting, scarce suppressed a scream: 380
'O stranger! in such hour of fear,
What evil hap has brought thee here?' —
'An evil hap how can it be
That bids me look again on thee?
By promise bound, my former guide   385
Met me betimes this morning tide,
And marshalled, over bank and bourne,[1]
The happy path of my return.' —
'The happy path! — what! said he naught
Of war, of battle to be fought,   390
Of guarded pass?' — 'No, by my faith!
Nor saw I aught could augur scathe.'[2] —
'O haste thee, Allan, to the kern,
— Yonder his tartans I discern;
Learn thou his purpose, and conjure[3]   395
That he will guide the stranger sure! —
What prompted thee, unhappy man?
The meanest serf in Roderick's clan
Had not been bribed by love or fear,
Unknown to him to guide thee here.'   400

XVII

'Sweet Ellen, dear my life must be,
Since it is worthy care from thee;

---

[1] Boundary.   [2] Predict harm.   [3] Solemnly entreat (him).

Yet life I hold but idle breath,
When love or honour's weighed with death.
Then let me profit by my chance,   405
And speak my purpose bold at once.
I come to bear thee from a wild
Where ne'er before such blossom smiled;
By this soft hand to lead thee far
From frantic scenes of feud and war.   410
Near Bochastle my horses wait;
They bear us soon to Stirling gate.
I'll place thee in a lovely bower,
I'll guard thee like a tender flower'—
'O! hush, Sir Knight! 'twere female art,[1]   415
To say I do not read thy heart;
Too much, before, my selfish ear
Was idly soothed my praise to hear.
That fatal bait hath lured thee back,
In deathful hour, o'er dangerous track;   420
And how, O how, can I atone
The wreck my vanity brought on!—
One way remains—I'll tell him all—
Yes! struggling bosom, forth it shall!
Thou, whose light folly bears the blame   425
Buy thine own pardon with thy shame!
But first—my father is a man
Outlawed and exiled, under ban;
The price of blood is on his head,
With me 'twere infamy to wed.—   430

[1] Deceit.

Still wouldst thou speak? — then hear the truth!
Fitz-James, there is a noble youth, —
If yet he is! — exposed for me
And mine to dread extremity —
Thou hast the secret of my heart;   435
Forgive, be generous, and depart!'

XVIII

Fitz-James knew every wily train[1]
A lady's fickle heart to gain;
But here he knew and felt them vain.
There shot no glance from Ellen's eye,   440
To give her steadfast speech the lie;
In maiden confidence she stood,
Though mantled in her cheek the blood,
And told her love with such a sigh
Of deep and hopeless agony,   445
As[2] death had sealed her Malcolm's doom,
And she sat sorrowing on his tomb.
Hope vanished from Fitz-James's eye,
But not with hope fled sympathy.
He proffered to attend her side,   450
As brother would a sister guide, —
'O! little know'st thou Roderick's heart!
Safer for both we go apart.
O haste thee, and from Allan learn
If thou mayst trust yon wily kern.'   455
With hand upon his forehead laid,

[1] Allurement.   [2] As if.

The conflict of his mind to shade,
A parting step or two he made;
Then, as some thought had crossed his brain,
He paused, and turned, and came again.   460

XIX

'Hear, lady, yet a parting word!—
It chanced in fight that my poor sword
Preserved the life of Scotland's lord.
This ring the grateful monarch gave,
And bade, when I had boon[1] to crave,   465
To bring it back, and boldly claim
The recompense that I would name.
Ellen, I am no courtly lord,
But one who lives by lance and sword,
Whose castle is his helm and shield,   470
His lordship[2] the embattled field.
What from a prince can I demand,
Who neither reck[3] of state nor land?
Ellen, thy hand—the ring is thine;
Each guard and usher knows the sign.   475
Seek thou the king without delay;
This signet shall secure thy way;
And claim thy suit, whate'er it be,
As ransom of his pledge to me.'
He placed the golden circlet on,   480
Paused—kissed her hand—and then was gone.
The aged minstrel stood aghast,

[1] Favour.   [2] Dominion.   [3] Care for.

So hastily Fitz-James shot past.
He joined his guide, and winding down
The ridges of the mountain brown,   485
Across the stream they took their way,
That joins Loch Katrine to Achray.

XX

All in the Trosachs' glen was still,
Noontide was sleeping on the hill:
Sudden his guide whooped loud and high — 490
' Murdoch! was that a signal cry?'—
He stammered forth — ' I shout to scare
Yon raven from his dainty fare.'
He looked — he knew the raven's prey,
His own brave steed: — 'Ah! gallant grey! 495
For thee — for me, perchance — 'twere well
We ne'er had seen the Trosachs' dell. —
Murdoch, move first — but silently;
Whistle or whoop, and thou shalt die!'
Jealous and sullen, on they fared,[1]   500
Each silent, each upon his guard.

XXI

Now wound the path its dizzy ledge
Around a precipice's edge,
When lo! a wasted female form,
Blighted by wrath of sun and storm,   505

---
[1] Went.

In tattered weeds [1] and wild array,
Stood on a cliff beside the way,
And glancing round her restless eye,
Upon the wood, the rock, the sky,
Seemed nought to mark, yet all to spy.　　510
Her brow was wreathed with gaudy broom;
With gesture wild she waved a plume
Of feathers, which the eagles fling
To crag and cliff from dusky wing;
Such spoils her desperate step had sought,　　515
Where scarce was footing for the goat.
The tartan plaid she first descried,
And shrieked till all the rocks replied;
As loud she laughed when near they drew,
For then the Lowland garb she knew;　　520
And then her hands she wildly wrung,
And then she wept, and then she sung —
She sung! — the voice, in better time,
Perchance to harp or lute might chime;
And now, though strained and roughened, still
Rung wildly sweet to dale and hill.　　526

XXII

SONG

'They bid me sleep, they bid me pray,
　　They say my brain is warped and wrung —
I cannot sleep on Highland brae,
　　I cannot pray in Highland tongue.　　530

[1] Clothes.

But were I now where Allan glides,
Or heard my native Devan's tides,
So sweetly would I rest, and pray
That Heaven would close my wintry day!

' 'Twas thus my hair they bade me braid,   535
    They made me to the church repair;
It was my bridal morn, they said,
    And my true love would meet me there.
But woe betide the cruel guile,
That drowned in blood the morning smile!   540
And woe betide the fairy dream!
I only waked to sob and scream.'

XXIII

'Who is this maid? what means her lay?
She hovers o'er the hollow way,
And flutters wide her mantle grey,   545
As the lone heron spreads his wing,
By twilight, o'er a haunted spring.' —
' 'Tis Blanche of Devan,' Murdoch said,
' A crazed and captive Lowland maid,
Ta'en on the morn she was a bride,   550
When Roderick forayed Devan-side.
The gay bridegroom resistance made,
And felt our chief's unconquered blade.
I marvel she is now at large,
But oft she 'scapes from Maudlin's charge. —   555

Hence, brain-sick fool!'—He raised his bow:—
'Now, if thou strikest her but one blow,
I'll pitch thee from the cliff as far
As ever peasant pitched a bar!'—
'Thanks, champion, thanks!' the maniac cried, 560
And pressed her to Fitz-James's side.
'See the grey pennons I prepare,
To seek my true-love through the air!
I will not lend that savage groom,
To break his fall, one downy plume! 565
No!—deep amid disjointed stones,
The wolves shall batten [1] on his bones,
And then shall his detested plaid,
By bush and brier in mid-air staid,
Wave forth a banner fair and free, 570
Meet signal for their revelry.'—

XXIV

'Hush thee, poor maiden, and be still!'—
'O! thou look'st kindly, and I will.—
Mine eye has dried and wasted been,
But still it loves the Lincoln green; 575
And, though mine ear is all unstrung,
Still, still it loves the Lowland tongue.

'For O my sweet William was forester true,
He stole poor Blanche's heart away!

[1] Fatten.

His coat it was all of the greenwood hue,   580
   And so blithely he trilled the Lowland lay!

' It was not that I meant to tell . . .
But thou art wise, and guessest well.'
Then, in a low and broken tone,
And hurried note, the song went on.   585
Still on the clansman fearfully
She fixed her apprehensive eye;
Then turned it on the knight, and then
Her look glanced wildly o'er the glen.

XXV

' The toils are pitched,[1] and the stakes are set,   590
   Ever sing merrily, merrily;
The bows they bend and the knives they whet,
   Hunters live so cheerily.

' It was a stag, a stag of ten,
   Bearing its branches sturdily;   595
He came stately down the glen,
   Ever sing hardily, hardily.

' It was there he met with a wounded doe,
   She was bleeding deathfully;
She warned him of the toils below,   600
   O, so faithfully, faithfully!

[1] Nets are set.

'He had an eye, and he could heed,
    Ever sing warily, warily ;
He had a foot, and he could speed —
    Hunters watch so narrowly.'   605

XXVI

Fitz-James's mind was passion-tossed,
When Ellen's hints and fears were lost ;
But Murdoch's shout suspicion wrought,
And Blanche's song conviction brought. —
Not like a stag that spies the snare,   610
But lion of the hunt aware,
He waved at once his blade on high,
'Disclose thy treachery, or die !'
Forth at full speed the clansman flew
But in his race his bow he drew.   615
The shaft just grazed Fitz-James's crest,
And thrilled[1] in Blanche's faded breast. —
Murdoch of Alpine ! prove thy speed,
For ne'er had Alpine's son such need !
With heart of fire, and foot of wind,   620
The fierce avenger is behind !
Fate judges of the rapid strife —
The forfeit death — the prize is life !
Thy kindred ambush lies before,
Close couched upon the heathery moor ;   625
Them couldst thou reach ! — it may not be —
Thine ambushed kin thou ne'er shalt see,

[1] Quivered.

The fiery Saxon gains on thee!
— Resistless speeds the deadly thrust,
As lightning strikes the pine to dust;   630
With foot and hand Fitz-James must strain,
Ere he can win his blade again.
Bent o'er the fallen, with falcon eye,
He grimly smiled to see him die;
Then slower wended back his way,   635
Where the poor maiden bleeding lay.

XXVII

She sat beneath the birchen tree,
Her elbow resting on her knee;
She had withdrawn the fatal shaft,
And gazed on it, and feebly laughed;   640
Her wreath of broom and feathers grey,
Daggled [1] with blood, beside her lay.
The knight to staunch the life-stream tried, —
' Stranger, it is in vain!' she cried.
' This hour of death has given me more   645
Of reason's power than years before;
For, as these ebbing veins decay,
My frenzied visions fade away.
A helpless injured wretch I die,
And something tells me in thine eye,   650
That thou wert my avenger born. —
Seest thou this tress? — O! still I've worn
This little tress of yellow hair,

[1] Wet.

Through danger, frenzy, and despair!
It once was bright and clear as thine,   655
But blood and tears have dimmed its shine.
I will not tell thee when 'twas shred,[1]
Nor from what guiltless victim's head —
My brain would turn! — but it shall wave
Like plumage on thy helmet brave,   660
Till sun and wind shall bleach the stain,
And thou wilt bring it me again. —
I waver still. —O God! more bright
Let reason beam her parting light! —
O! by thy knighthood's honoured sign,   665
And for thy life preserved by mine,
When thou shalt see a darksome man,
Who boasts him chief of Alpine's clan,
With tartans broad, and shadowy plume,
And hand of blood, and brow of gloom,   670
Be thy heart bold, thy weapon strong,
And wreak[2] poor Blanche of Devan's wrong!
They watch for thee by pass and fell . . .
Avoid the path . . . O God! . . . farewell.'

XXVIII

A kindly heart had brave Fitz-James;   675
Fast poured his eyes at pity's claims;
And now with mingled grief and ire,
He saw the murdered maid expire.
'God, in my need, be my relief,

----
[1] Cut.   [2] Avenge.

As I wreak this on yonder chief!'   680
A lock from Blanche's tresses fair
He blended with her bridegroom's hair;
The mingled braid in blood he dyed,
And placed it on his bonnet-side:
'By Him whose word is truth, I swear,   685
No other favour [1] will I wear,
Till this sad token I imbrue [2]
In the best blood of Roderick Dhu.
— But hark! what means yon faint halloo?
The chase is up, — but they shall know   690
The stag at bay's a dangerous foe.'
Barred from the known but guarded way,
Through copse and cliffs Fitz-James must stray,
And oft must change his desperate track,
By stream and precipice turned back.   695
Heartless, fatigued, and faint, at length,
From lack of food and loss of strength,
He couched him [3] in a thicket hoar,
And thought his toils and perils o'er: —
'Of all my rash adventurous past,   700
This frantic feat must prove the last!
Who e'er so mad but might have guess'd,
That all this Highland hornet's nest
Would muster up in swarms so soon
As e'er they heard of bands at Doune?   705
Like bloodhounds now they search me out, —
Hark, to the whistle and the shout! —

---

[1] Token from a lady.   [2] Soak.   [3] Lay down.

If farther through the wilds I go,
I only fall upon the foe :
I'll couch me here till evening grey,
Then darkling try my dangerous way.'

XXIX

The shades of eve come slowly down,
The woods are wrapt in deeper brown,
The owl awakens from her dell,
The fox is heard upon the fell ;   715
Enough remains of glimmering light
To guide the wanderer's steps aright,
Yet not enough from far to show
His figure to the watchful foe.
With cautious step, and ear awake,   720
He climbs the crag and threads the brake ;
And not the summer solstice there
Tempered the midnight mountain air,
But every breeze that swept the wold
Benumbed his drenched limbs with cold.   725
In dread, in danger, and alone,
Famished and chilled, through ways unknown,
Tangled and steep, he journeyed on ;
Till, as a rock's huge point he turned,
A watch-fire close before him burned.   730

XXX

Beside its embers red and clear,
Basked, in his plaid, a mountaineer ;

And up he sprung with sword in hand, —
'Thy name and purpose?   Saxon, stand!' —
'A stranger.' — 'What dost thou require?' — 735
'Rest and a guide, and food and fire.
My life's beset, my path is lost,
The gale has chilled my limbs with frost.' —
'Art thou a friend to Roderick?' — 'No.' —
'Thou darest not call thyself a foe?' —   740
'I dare! to him and all the band
He brings to aid his murderous hand.' —
'Bold words! — but, though the beast of game
The privilege of chase may claim,
Though space and law the stag we lend,   745
Ere hound we slip,[1] or bow we bend,
Who ever recked where, how, or when,
The prowling fox was trapped or slain?
Thus treacherous scouts, — yet sure they lie,
Who say thou camest a secret spy!' —   750
'They do, by heaven! — Come Roderick Dhu,
And of his clan the boldest two,
And let me but till morning rest,
I write the falsehood on their crest.' —
'If by the blaze I mark aright,   755
Thou bear'st the belt and spur of knight.' —
'Then by these tokens mayest thou know
Each proud oppressor's mortal foe.' —
'Enough, enough; — sit down, and share
A soldier's couch, a soldier's fare.'   760

[1] Let loose.

XXXI

He gave him of his Highland cheer,
The hardened flesh of mountain deer;
Dry fuel on the fire he laid,
And bade the Saxon share his plaid.
He tended him like welcome guest,   765
Then thus his further speech addressed: --
' Stranger, I am to Roderick Dhu
A clansman born, a kinsman true;
Each word against his honour spoke
Demands of me avenging stroke;   770
Yet more, upon thy fate, 'tis said,
A mighty augury is laid.
It rests with me to wind my horn, --
Thou art with numbers overborne;
It rests with me, here, brand to brand,   775
Worn as thou art, to bid thee stand:
But, not for clan, nor kindred's cause,
Will I depart from honour's laws;
To assail a wearied man were shame,
And stranger is a holy name;   780
Guidance and rest, and food and fire,
In vain he never must require.
Then rest thee here till dawn of day;
Myself will guide thee on the way,
O'er stock[1] and stone, through watch and ward,
Till past Clan-Alpine's utmost guard,   785

[1] Stump.

As far as Coilantogle's ford;
From thence thy warrant is thy sword.' —
'I take thy courtesy, by heaven,
As freely as 'tis nobly given!'—   790
'Well, rest thee; for the bittern's cry
Sings us the lake's wild lullaby.'
With that he shook the gathered heath,
And spread his plaid upon the wreath;
And the brave foemen, side by side,   795
Lay peaceful down, like brothers tried,
And slept until the dawning beam
Purpled the mountain and the stream.

CANTO FIFTH

The Combat

I

Fair as the earliest beam of eastern light,
  When first, by the bewildered pilgrim spied,
It smiles upon the dreary brow of night,
  And silvers o'er the torrent's foaming tide,
And lights the fearful path on mountain side; —   5
  Fair as that beam, although the fairest far,
Giving to horror grace, to danger pride,
  Shine martial Faith, and Courtesy's bright star,
Through all the wreckful storms that cloud the brow of
    War.

II

  That early beam, so fair and sheen,   10
  Was twinkling through the hazel screen,
  When, rousing at its glimmer red,
  The warriors left their lowly bed,
  Looked out upon the dappled sky,
  Muttered their soldier matins by,   15
  And then awaked their fire, to steal,
  As short and rude, their soldier meal.
  That o'er, the Gael around him threw
  His graceful plaid of varied hue,

And, true to promise, led the way,20
By thicket green and mountain grey.
A wildering path!—they winded now
Along the precipice's brow,
Commanding the rich scenes beneath,
The windings of the Forth and Teith,25
And all the vales between that lie,
Till Stirling's turrets melt in sky;
Then, sunk in copse, their farthest glance
Gained not the length of horseman's lance.
'Twas oft so steep, the foot was fain30
Assistance from the hand to gain;
So tangled oft, that, bursting through,
Each hawthorn shed her showers of dew,—
That diamond dew, so pure and clear,
It rivals all but Beauty's tear!35

III

At length they came where, stern and steep,
The hill sinks down upon the deep.
Here Vennachar in silver flows,
There, ridge on ridge, Benledi rose;
Ever the hollow path twined on,40
Beneath steep bank and threatening stone;
An hundred men might hold the post
With hardihood against a host.
The rugged mountain's scanty cloak
Was dwarfish shrubs of birch and oak,45

With shingles [1] bare, and cliffs between,
And patches bright of bracken green,
And heather black, that waved so high,
It held the copse in rivalry.
But where the lake slept deep and still,   50
Dank osiers [2] fringed the swamp and hill;
And oft both path and hill were torn,
Where wintry torrent down had borne,
And heaped upon the cumbered land
Its wreck of gravel, rocks, and sand.   55
So toilsome was the road to trace,
The guide, abating of his pace,
Led slowly through the pass's jaws,
And asked Fitz-James, by what strange cause
He sought these wilds, traversed by few,   60
Without a pass from Roderick Dhu.

IV

'Brave Gael, my pass in danger tried,
Hangs in my belt, and by my side;
Yet, sooth to tell,' the Saxon said,
'I dreamt not now to claim its aid.   65
When here, but three days since, I came,
Bewildered in pursuit of game,
All seemed as peaceful and as still
As the mist slumbering on yon hill;
Thy dangerous chief was then afar,   70
Nor soon expected back from war.

[1] Gravelly places.   [2] Willows.

Thus said, at least, my mountain-guide,
Though deep, perchance, the villain lied.' —
' Yet why a second venture try ? ' —
' A warrior thou, and ask me why ! —   75
Moves our free course by such fixed cause
As gives the poor mechanic laws ?
Enough, I sought to drive away
The lazy hours of peaceful day ;
Slight cause will then suffice to guide   80
A knight's free footsteps far and wide, —
A falcon flown, a greyhound strayed,
The merry glance of mountain maid :
Or, if a path be dangerous known,
The danger's self is lure alone.' —   85

V

' Thy secret keep, I urge thee not ; —
Yet, ere again ye sought this spot,
Say, heard ye nought of Lowland war,
Against Clan-Alpine, raised by Mar ? '
— ' No, by my word ; — of bands prepared   90
To guard King James's sports I heard ;
Nor doubt I aught, but, when they hear
This muster of the mountaineer,
Their pennons will abroad be flung,
Which else in Doune had peaceful hung.' —   95
' Free be they flung ! — for we were loath
Their silken folds should feast the moth.

Free be they flung!—as free shall wave
Clan-Alpine's Pine in banner brave.
But, stranger, peaceful since you came,   100
Bewildered in the mountain game,
Whence the bold boast by which you show
Vich-Alpine's vowed and mortal foe?'—
'Warrior, but yester-morn I knew
Naught of thy chieftain, Roderick Dhu,   105
Save as an outlawed desperate man,
The chief of a rebellious clan,
Who, in the Regent's court and sight,
With ruffian dagger stabbed a knight:
Yet this alone might from his part   110
Sever each true and loyal heart.'

VI

Wrothful at such arraignment foul,
Dark lowered the clansman's sable scowl.
A space he paused, then sternly said,
'And heardst thou why he drew his blade?   115
Heardst thou that shameful word and blow
Brought Roderick's vengeance on his foe?
What recked the chieftain if he stood
On Highland heath or Holy-Rood?
He rights such wrong where it is given,   120
If it were in the court of heaven.'—
'Still was it outrage;—yet, 'tis true,
Not then claimed sovereignty his due;

While Albany, with feeble hand,
Held borrowed truncheon[1] of command,   125
The young king, mewed[2] in Stirling tower,
Was stranger to respect and power.
But then, thy chieftain's robber life!—
Winning mean prey by causeless strife,
Wrenching from ruined Lowland swain   130
His herds and harvest reared in vain.—
Methinks a soul like thine should scorn
The spoils from such foul foray borne.'

VII

The Gael beheld him grim the while,
And answered with disdainful smile,—   135
'Saxon, from yonder mountain high,
I marked thee send delighted eye,
Far to the south and east, where lay,
Extended in succession gay,
Deep waving fields and pastures green,   140
With gentle slopes and groves between:—
These fertile plains, that softened vale.
Were once the birthright of the Gael;
The stranger came with iron hand,
And from our fathers reft the land.   145
Where dwell we now? See, rudely swell
Crag over crag, and fell o'er fell.
Ask we this savage hill we tread

---

[1] Mace (symbol of authority).   [2] Shut up.

For fattened steer or household bread;
Ask we for flocks these shingles dry,   150
And well the mountain might reply, —
" To you, as to your sires of yore,
Belong the target [1] and claymore !
I give you shelter in my breast,
Your own good blades must win the rest."   155
Pent in this fortress of the North,
Think'st thou we will not sally forth,
To spoil the spoiler as we may,
And from the robber rend the prey?
Ay, by my soul ! — While on yon plain   160
The Saxon rears [2] one shock of grain;
While of ten thousand herds there strays
But one along yon river's maze, —
The Gael, of plain and river heir,
Shall, with strong hand, redeem his share.   165
Where live the mountain chiefs who hold,
That plundering Lowland field and fold
Is aught but retribution true?
Seek other cause 'gainst Roderick Dhu.' —

VIII

Answered Fitz-James, — ' And, if I sought,   170
Think'st thou no other could be brought?
What deem ye of my path waylaid?
My life given o'er to ambuscade?' —

---

[1] Round shield.   [2] Raises.

'As of a meed[1] to rashness due:
Hadst thou sent warning fair and true, —   175
I seek my hound, or falcon staid,
I seek, good faith, a Highland maid, —
Free hadst thou been to come and go;
But secret path marks secret foe.
Nor yet, for this, even as a spy,   180
Hadst thou, unheard, been doomed to die,
Save to fulfil an augury.' —
'Well, let it pass; nor will I now
Fresh cause of enmity avow,
To chafe my mood and cloud thy brow.   185
Enough, I am by promise tied
To match me with this man of pride:
Twice have I sought Clan-Alpine's glen
In peace; but when I come again,
I come with banner, brand, and bow,   190
As leader seeks his mortal foe.
For love-lorn swain in lady's bower
Ne'er panted for the appointed hour,
As I, until before me stand
This rebel chieftain and his band!' —   195

IX

'Have then thy wish!' — He whistled shrill,
And he was answered from the hill;
Wild as the scream of the curlew,

[1] Reward.

From crag to crag the signal flew.
Instant, through copse and heath, arose   200
Bonnets and spears and bended bows;
On right, on left, above, below,
Sprung up at once the lurking foe;
From shingles grey their lances start,
The bracken bush sends forth the dart,   205
The rushes and the willow-wand
Are bristling into ax and brand,
And every tuft of broom gives life
To plaided warrior armed for strife.
That whistle garrisoned the glen   210
At once with full five hundred men,
As if the yawning hill to heaven
A subterranean host had given.
Watching their leader's beck and will,
All silent there they stood, and still.   215
Like the loose crags, whose threatening mass
Lay tottering o'er the hollow pass,
As if an infant's touch could urge
Their headlong passage down the verge,
With step and weapon forward flung,   220
Upon the mountain-side they hung.
The mountaineer cast glance of pride
Along Benledi's living side,
Then fixed his eye and sable brow
Full on Fitz-James — ' How say'st thou now? 225
These are Clan-Alpine's warriors true;
And, Saxon, — I am Roderick Dhu!'

X

Fitz-James was brave : — though to his heart
The life-blood thrilled with sudden start,
He manned himself with dauntless air,   230
Returned the chief his haughty stare,
His back against a rock he bore,
And firmly placed his foot before : —
'Come one, come all ! this rock shall fly
From its firm base as soon as I.'   235
Sir Roderick marked — and in his eyes
Respect was mingled with surprise,
And the stern joy which warriors feel
In foeman worthy of their steel.
Short space he stood — then waved his hand : 240
Down sunk the disappearing band ;
Each warrior vanished where he stood,
In broom or bracken, heath or wood ;
Sunk brand and spear and bended bow,
In osiers pale and copses low ;   245
It seemed as if their mother Earth
Had swallowed up her warlike birth.
The wind's last breath had tossed in air
Pennon and plaid and plumage fair, —
The next but swept a lone hill-side,   250
Where heath and fern were waving wide :
The sun's last glance was glinted [1] back
From spear and glaive, from targe and jack,[2] —

---

[1] Flashed.   [2] Horseman's jacket.

The next, all unreflected, shone
On bracken green, and cold grey stone.   255

XI

Fitz-James looked round — yet scarce believed
The witness that his sight received;
Such apparition well might seem
Delusion of a dreadful dream.
Sir Roderick in suspense he eyed,   260
And to his look the chief replied:
' Fear naught — nay, that I need not say —
But — doubt not aught from mine array.
Thou art my guest; — I pledged my word
As far as Coilantogle ford: 265
Nor would I call a clansman's brand
For aid against one valiant hand,
Though on our strife lay [1] every vale
Rent by the Saxon from the Gael.
So move we on; — I only meant   270
To show the reed on which you leant,
Deeming this path you might pursue
Without a pass from Roderick Dhu.'
They moved: — I said Fitz-James was brave
As ever knight that belted glaive;   275
Yet dare not say that now his blood
Kept on its wont [2] and tempered flood,
As, following Roderick's stride, he drew
That seeming lonesome pathway through,

---

[1] Depended.   [2] Usual.

Which yet, by fearful proof, was rife   280
With lances, that, to take his life,
Waited but signal from a guide
So late dishonour'd and defied.
Ever, by stealth, his eye sought round
The vanished guardians of the ground,   285
And still, from copse and heather deep,
Fancy saw spear and broadsword peep,
And in the plover's shrilly strain
The signal-whistle heard again.
Nor breathed he free till far behind   290
The pass was left; for then they wind
Along a wide and level green,
Where neither tree nor tuft was seen,
Nor rush nor bush of broom was near,
To hide a bonnet or a spear.   295

XII

The chief in silence strode before,
And reached that torrent's sounding shore,
Which, daughter of three mighty lakes,
From Vennachar in silver breaks,
Sweeps through the plain, and ceaseless mines 300
On Bochastle the mouldering lines,
Where Rome, the empress of the world,
Of yore her eagle wings unfurled.
And here his course the chieftain staid,
Threw down his target and his plaid,   305
And to the Lowland warrior said —

LADY OF THE LAKE — 12

'Bold Saxon! to his promise just,
Vich-Alpine has discharged his trust.
This murderous chief, this ruthless man,
This head of a rebellious clan,   310
Hath led thee safe, through watch and ward,
Far past Clan-Alpine's outmost guard.
Now, man to man, and steel to steel,
A chieftain's vengeance thou shalt feel.
See, here all vantageless[1] I stand,   315
Armed, like thyself, with single brand:
For this is Coilantogle ford,
And thou must keep thee with thy sword.'

XIII

The Saxon paused:—'I ne'er delayed,
When foeman bade me draw my blade;   320
Nay, more, brave chief, I vowed thy death:
Yet sure thy fair and generous faith,
And my deep debt for life preserved,
A better meed have well deserved:
Can naught but blood our feud atone?   325
Are there no means?'—'No, stranger, none!
And hear,—to fire thy flagging zeal,—
The Saxon cause rests on thy steel;
For thus spoke Fate, by prophet bred
Between the living and the dead: 330
"Who spills the foremost foeman's life,
His party conquers in the strife."'—

[1] Without advantage.

'Then, by my word,' the Saxon said,
'The riddle is already read.
Seek yonder brake beneath the cliff,—   335
There lies Red Murdoch, stark and stiff.
Thus Fate has solved her prophecy;
Then yield to Fate, and not to me.
To James, at Stirling, let us go,
When, if thou wilt be still his foe,   340
Or if the king shall not agree
To grant thee grace and favour free,
I plight mine honour, oath, and word,
That, to thy native strengths[1] restored,
With each advantage shalt thou stand,   345
That aids thee now to guard thy land.'

XIV

Dark lightning flashed from Roderick's eye—
'Soars thy presumption, then, so high,
Because a wretched kern ye slew,
Homage to name to Roderick Dhu?   350
He yields not, he, to man nor Fate!
Thou add'st but fuel to my hate:—
My clansman's blood demands revenge.
Not yet prepared?—By Heaven, I change
My thought, and hold thy valour light   355
As that of some vain carpet knight,
Who ill deserved my courteous care,
And whose best boast is but to wear

[1] Forces.

A braid of his fair lady's hair.'—
'I thank thee, Roderick, for the word!   360
It nerves my heart, it steels my sword;
For I have sworn this braid to stain
In the best blood that warms thy vein.
Now, truce, farewell! and, ruth,[1] begone!—
Yet think not that by thee alone,   365
Proud chief! can courtesy be shown;
Though not from copse, or heath, or cairn,[2]
Start at my whistle clansmen stern,
Of this small horn one feeble blast
Would fearful odds against thee cast.   370
But fear not — doubt not — which thou wilt —
We try this quarrel hilt to hilt.' —
Then each at once his falchion drew,
Each on the ground his scabbard threw,
Each looked to sun, and stream, and plain,   375
As what they ne'er might see again;
Then, foot and point and eye opposed,
In dubious strife they darkly closed.

XV

Ill fared it then with Roderick Dhu,
That on the field his targe he threw,   380
Whose brazen studs and tough bull-hide
Had death so often dashed aside;
For, trained abroad his arms to wield,

---

[1] Pity.   [2] Heap of stones.

Fitz-James's blade was sword and shield.
He practised every pass and ward,[1]   385
To thrust, to strike, to feint, to guard;
While less expert, though stronger far,
The Gael maintained unequal war.
Three times in closing strife they stood,
And thrice the Saxon blade drank blood;   390
No stinted draught, no scanty tide,
The gushing flood the tartans dyed.
Fierce Roderick felt the fatal drain,
And showered his blows like wintry rain;
And, as firm rock or castle-roof   395
Against the winter shower is proof,
The foe, invulnerable still,
Foiled his wild rage by steady skill;
Till, at advantage ta'en, his brand
Forced Roderick's weapon from his hand,   400
And backward borne upon the lea,
Brought the proud chieftain to his knee.

XVI

'Now, yield thee, or by Him who made
The world, thy heart's blood dyes my blade!'—
'Thy threats, thy mercy, I defy!   405
Let recreant yield, who fears to die.'
— Like adder darting from his coil,
Like wolf that dashes through the toil,

[1] Attack and defence.

Like mountain-cat who guards her young,
Full at Fitz-James's throat he sprung ;   410
Received, but recked not of a wound,
And locked his arms his foeman round. —
Now, gallant Saxon, hold thine own !
No maiden's hand is round thee thrown !
That desperate grasp thy frame might feel   415
Through bars of brass and triple steel ! —
They tug, they strain ! down, down they go,
The Gael above, Fitz-James below.
The chieftain's gripe his throat compressed,
His knee was planted in his breast ;   420
His clotted locks he backward threw,
Across his brow his hand he drew,
From blood and mist to clear his sight,
Then gleamed aloft his dagger bright ! —
— But hate and fury ill supplied   425
The stream of life's exhausted tide,
And all too late the advantage came,
To turn the odds of deadly game ;
For, while the dagger gleamed on high,
Reeled soul and sense, reeled brain and eye.   430
Down came the blow ! but in the heath
The erring blade found bloodless sheath.
The struggling foe may now unclasp
The fainting chief's relaxing grasp ;
Unwounded from the dreadful close,[1]   435
But breathless all, Fitz-James arose.

[1] Encounter.

XVII

He faltered thanks to Heaven for life,
Redeemed, unhoped, from desperate strife;
Next on his foe his look he cast,
Whose every gasp appeared his last;　　　440
In Roderick's gore he dipt the braid, —
'Poor Blanche! thy wrongs are dearly paid:
Yet with thy foe must die, or live,
The praise that faith and valour give.'
With that he blew a bugle-note,　　　445
Undid the collar from his throat,
Unbonneted, and by the wave
Sat down his brow and hands to lave.
Then faint afar are heard the feet
Of rushing steeds in gallop fleet;　　　450
The sounds increase, and now are seen
Four mounted squires in Lincoln green;
Two who bear lance, and two who lead
By loosened rein a saddled steed;
Each onward held his headlong course,　　　455
And by Fitz-James reined up his horse;
With wonder viewed the bloody spot —
— 'Exclaim not, gallants! question not. —
You, Herbert and Luffness, alight,
And bind the wounds of yonder knight;　　　460
Let the grey palfrey bear his weight,
We destined for a fairer freight,
And bring him on to Stirling straight;

I will before at better speed,
To seek fresh horse and fitting weed.[1]   465
The sun rides high ; — I must be boune,
To see the archer-game at noon ;
But lightly Bayard clears the lea. —
De Vaux and Herries, follow me.

XVIII

' Stand, Bayard, stand ! ' — the steed obeyed, 470
With arching neck and bended head,
And glancing eye and quivering ear,
As if he loved his lord to hear.
No foot Fitz-James in stirrup staid,
No grasp upon the saddle laid,   475
But wreathed his left hand in the mane,
And lightly bounded from the plain,
Turned on the horse his armed heel,
And stirred his courage with the steel.
Bounded the fiery steed in air,   480
The rider sat erect and fair,
Then like a bolt from steel crossbow
Forth launched, along the plain they go.
They dashed that rapid torrent through,
And up Carhonie's hill they flew ;   485
Still at the gallop pricked[2] the knight,
His merry-men followed as they might.
Along thy banks, swift Teith ! they ride,
And in the race they mock thy tide ;

[1] Clothing.   [2] Spurred on.

Torry and Lendrick now are past,   490
And Deanstown lies behind them cast;
They rise, the bannered towers of Doune,
They sink in distant woodland soon;
Blair-Drummond sees the hoofs strike fire,
They sweep like breeze through Ochtertyre;   495
They mark just glance and disappear
The lofty brow of ancient Kier;
They bathe their coursers' sweltering sides,
Dark Forth! amid thy sluggish tides,
And on the opposing shore take ground,   500
With plash, with scramble, and with bound.
Right-hand they leave thy cliffs, Craig-Forth!
And soon the bulwark of the North,
Grey Stirling, with her towers and town,
Upon their fleet career looked down.   505

XIX

As up the flinty path they strained,
Sudden his steed the leader reined;
A signal to his squire he flung,
Who instant to his stirrup sprung:—
'Seest thou, De Vaux, yon woodsman grey,   510
Who townward holds the rocky way,
Of stature tall and poor array?
Mark'st thou the firm, yet active stride,
With which he scales the mountain-side?
Know'st thou from whence he comes, or whom?'   515
'No, by my word;—a burly groom

He seems, who in the field or chase
A baron's train would nobly grace.' —
'Out, out, De Vaux! can fear supply,
And jealousy, no sharper eye?   520
Afar, ere to the hill he drew,
That stately form and step I knew;
Like form in Scotland is not seen,
Treads not such step on Scottish green.
'Tis James of Douglas, by Saint Serle!   525
The uncle of the banished Earl.
Away, away, to court, to show
The near approach of dreaded foe:
The king must stand upon his guard;
Douglas and he must meet prepared.'   530
Then right-hand wheeled their steeds, and straight
They won the castle's postern gate.[1]

XX

The Douglas, who had bent his way
From Cambus-Kenneth's abbey grey,
Now, as he climbed the rocky shelf,   535
Held sad communion with himself: —
'Yes! all is true my fears could frame;
A prisoner lies the noble Græme,
And fiery Roderick soon will feel
The vengeance of the royal steel.   540
I, only I, can ward their fate, —
God grant the ransom come not late!

[1] Back, or private, gate.

The abbess hath her promise given,
My child shall be the bride of Heaven; —
— Be pardoned one repining tear! 545
For He who gave her knows how dear,
How excellent! but that is by,[1]
And now my business is — to die.
— Ye towers! within whose circuit dread
A Douglas by his sovereign bled; 550
And thou, O sad and fatal mound!
That oft hast heard the death-ax sound,
As on the noblest of the land
Fell the stern headsman's bloody hand, —
The dungeon, block, and nameless tomb 555
Prepare — for Douglas seeks his doom!
— But hark! what blithe and jolly peal
Makes the Franciscan steeple reel?
And see! upon the crowded street,
In motley groups what maskers meet! 560
Banner and pageant, pipe and drum,
And merry morrice-dancers come.
I guess, by all this quaint array,
The burghers[2] hold their sports to-day.
James will be there; he loves such show, 565
Where the good yeoman bends his bow,
And the tough wrestler foils his foe,
As well as where, in proud career,
The high-born tilter[3] shivers spear.
I'll follow to the castle-park, 570

[1] Past.   [2] Citizens.   [3] Contestant in a tournament.

And play my prize ; — King James shall mark
If age has tamed these sinews stark,
Whose force so oft, in happier days,
His boyish wonder loved to praise.'

XXI

The castle gates were open flung,   575
The quivering drawbridge rocked and rung,
And echoed loud the flinty street
Beneath the coursers' clattering feet,
As slowly down the steep descent
Fair Scotland's king and nobles went,   580
While all along the crowded way
Was jubilee and loud huzza.
And ever James was bending low
To his white jennet's[1] saddle-bow,
Doffing his cap to city dame,   585
Who smiled and blushed for pride and shame.
And well the simperer might be vain, —
He chose the fairest of the train.
Gravely he greets each city sire,
Commends each pageant's quaint attire,   590
Gives to the dancers thanks aloud,
And smiles and nods upon the crowd,
Who rend the heavens with their acclaims —
'Long live the Commons' king, King James!'
Behind the king thronged peer and knight,   595
And noble dame, and damsel bright,

[1] Spanish horse.

Whose fiery steeds ill brooked the stay
Of the steep street and crowded way.
— But in the train you might discern
Dark lowering brow, and visage stern :   600
There nobles mourned their pride restrained,
And the mean burgher's joys disdained ;
And chiefs, who, hostage for their clan,
Were each from home a banished man,
There thought upon their own grey tower,   605
Their waving woods, their feudal power,
And deemed themselves a shameful part
Of pageant which they cursed in heart.

XXII

Now, in the castle-park, drew out
Their chequered bands the joyous rout.   610
Their morricers, with bell at heel
And blade in hand, their mazes wheel ;
But chief, beside the butts,[1] there stand
Bold Robin Hood and all his band, —
Friar Tuck with quarterstaff[2] and cowl,   615
Old Scathelocke with his surly scowl,
Maid Marian, fair as ivory bone,
Scarlet, and Mutch, and Little John ;
Their bugles challenge all that will,
In archery to prove their skill.   620
The Douglas bent a bow of might, —
His first shaft centred in the white,

---

[1] Marks to shoot at.   [2] Pole.

And when in turn he shot again,
His second split the first in twain.
From the king's hand must Douglas **take**   625
A silver dart, the archer's stake[1];
Fondly he watched, with watery eye,
Some answering glance of sympathy, —
No kind emotion made reply!
Indifferent as to archer wight,[2]   630
The monarch gave the arrow bright.

XXIII

Now, clear the ring! for, hand to hand,
The manly wrestlers take their stand.
Two o'er the rest superior rose,
And proud demanded mightier foes,   635
Nor called in vain; for Douglas came.
— For life is Hugh of Larbert lame;
Scarce better John of Alloa's fare,
Whom senseless home his comrades bear.
Prize of the wrestling match, the king   640
To Douglas gave a golden ring,
While coldly glanced his eye of blue,
As frozen drop of wintry dew.
Douglas would speak, but in his breast
His struggling soul his words suppressed;   645
Indignant then he turned him where
Their arms the brawny yeomen bare,

---

[1] Prize.   [2] *I.e.*, an ordinary archer.

To hurl the massive bar in air.
When each his utmost strength had shown,
The Douglas rent an earth-fast stone   650
From its deep bed, then heaved it high,
And sent the fragment through the sky,
A rood beyond the farthest mark; —
And still in Stirling's royal park,
The grey-haired sires, who know the past,   655
To strangers point the Douglas cast,
And moralize on the decay
Of Scottish strength in modern day.

XXIV

The vale with loud applauses rang,
The Ladies' Rock sent back the clang.   660
The king, with look unmoved, bestowed
A purse well filled with pieces broad,
Indignant smiled the Douglas proud,
And threw the gold among the crowd,
Who now with anxious wonder scan,   665
And sharper glance, the dark grey man;
Till whispers rose among the throng,
That heart so free, and hand so strong,
Must to the Douglas blood belong.
The old men marked, and shook the head,   670
To see his hair with silver spread,
And winked aside, and told each son
Of feats upon the English done,

Ere Douglas of the stalwart hand
Was exiled from his native land.   675
The women praised his stately form,
Though wrecked by many a winter's storm;
The youth with awe and wonder saw
His strength surpassing nature's law.
Thus judged, as is their wont, the crowd,   680
Till murmur rose to clamours loud.
But not a glance from that proud ring
Of peers who circled round the king
With Douglas held communion kind,
Or called the banished man to mind;   685
No, not from those who, at the chase,
Once held his side the honoured place,
Begirt his board, and in the field
Found safety underneath his shield;
For he whom royal eyes disown,   690
When was his form to courtiers known!

XXV

The monarch saw the gambols flag,
And bade let loose a gallant stag,
Whose pride, the holiday to crown,
Two favourite greyhounds should pull down.   695
That venison free, and Bourdeaux wine,
Might serve the archery [1] to dine.
But Lufra, — whom from Douglas' side

[1] Company of archers.

Nor bribe nor threat could e'er divide,
The fleetest hound in all the North,—   700
Brave Lufra saw, and darted forth.
She left the royal hounds mid-way,
And dashing on the antlered prey,
Sunk her sharp muzzle in his flank,
And deep the flowing life-blood drank.   705
The king's stout huntsman saw the sport
By strange intruder broken short,
Came up, and with his leash unbound,
In anger struck the noble hound.
—The Douglas had endured, that morn,   710
The king's cold look, the nobles' scorn,
And last, and worst to spirit proud,
Had borne the pity of the crowd;
But Lufra had been fondly bred,.
To share his board, to watch his bed,   715
And oft would Ellen Lufra's neck
In maiden glee with garlands deck;
They were such playmates, that with name
Of Lufra Ellen's image came.
His stifled wrath is brimming high,   720
In darkened brow and flashing eye;
As waves before the bark divide,
The crowd gave way before his stride;
Needs but a buffet and no more,—
The groom lies senseless in his gore.   725
Such blow no other hand could deal,
Though gauntleted in glove of steel.

XXVI

Then clamoured loud the royal train,
And brandished swords and staves amain.
But stern the baron's warning — ' Back !   730
Back, on your lives, ye menial pack !
Beware the Douglas. — Yes ! behold,
King James ! the Douglas, doomed of old,
And vainly sought for near and far,
A victim to atone the war,   735
A willing victim, now attends,
Nor craves thy grace but for his friends.'
' Thus is my clemency repaid ?
Presumptuous lord ! ' the monarch said ;
' Of thy mis-proud ambitious clan,   740
Thou, James of Bothwell, wert the man,
The only man, in whom a foe
My woman-mercy would not know :
But shall a monarch's presence brook
Injurious blow and haughty look ? —   745
What ho ! the captain of our Guard !
Give the offender fitting ward.[1] —
Break off the sports ! ' — for tumult rose,
And yeomen 'gan to bend their bows, —
' Break off the sports ! ' he said, and frowned, 750
' And bid our horsemen clear the ground.'

XXVII

Then uproar **wild** and misarray[2]
Marred the fair form of festal day.

[1] Guard, confinement.   [2] Disorder.

The horsemen pricked among the crowd.
Repelled by threats and insult loud;   755
To earth are borne the old and weak,
The timorous fly, the women shriek;
With flint, with shaft, with staff, with bar,
The hardier urge [1] tumultuous war.
At once round Douglas darkly sweep   760
The royal spears in circle deep,
And slowly scale the pathway steep;
While on the rear in thunder pour
The rabble with disordered roar.
With grief the noble Douglas saw   765
The Commons rise against the law,
And to the leading soldier said, —
' Sir John of Hyndford ! 'twas my blade
That knighthood on thy shoulder laid;
For that good deed, permit me then   770
A word with these misguided men.—

XXVIII

' Hear, gentle friends ! ere yet for me
Ye break the bands of fealty.[2]
My life, my honour, and my cause,
I tender free to Scotland's laws.   775
Are these so weak as must require
The aid of your misguided ire?
Or, if I suffer causeless wrong,
Is then my selfish rage so strong,

---

[1] Carry on.   [2] Allegiance.

My sense of public weal so low,   780
That, for mean vengeance on a foe,
Those cords of love I should unbind
Which knit my country and my kind?[1]
O no! Believe, in yonder tower
It will not soothe my captive hour,   785
To know those spears our foes should dread
For me in kindred gore are red;
To know, in fruitless brawl begun
For me that mother wails her son,
For me that widow's mate expires,   790
For me that orphans weep their sires,
That patriots mourn insulted laws,
And curse the Douglas for the cause.
O let your patience ward[2] such ill,
And keep your right to love me still!'   795

XXIX

The crowd's wild fury sunk again
In tears, as tempests melt in rain.
With lifted hands and eyes, they prayed
For blessings on his generous head,
Who for his country felt alone   800
And prized her blood beyond his own.
Old men, upon the verge of life,
Blessed him who staid the civil strife;
And mothers held their babes on high,
The self-devoted chief to spy,   805

[1] Race.   [2] Guard against.

Triumphant over wrongs and ire,
To whom the prattlers owed a sire:
Even the rough soldier's heart was moved;
As if behind some bier beloved,
With trailing arms and drooping head,   810
The Douglas up the hill he led,
And at the castle's battled[1] verge
With sighs resigned his honoured charge.

XXX

The offended monarch rode apart,
With bitter thought and swelling heart,   815
And would not now vouchsafe again
Through Stirling streets to lead his train. —
'O Lennox, who would wish to rule
This changeling crowd, this common fool?
Hear'st thou,' he said, ' the loud acclaim,   820
With which they shout the Douglas name?
With like acclaim, the vulgar throat
Strained for King James their morning note;
With like acclaim they hailed the day
When first I broke the Douglas sway;   825
And like acclaim would Douglas greet,
If he could hurl me from my seat.
Who o'er the herd would wish to reign,
Fantastic, fickle, fierce, and vain!
Vain as the leaf upon the stream,   830
And fickle as a changeful dream;

[1] Strengthened with battlements.

Fantastic as a woman's mood,
And fierce as Frenzy's fevered blood,
Thou many-headed monster-thing,
O who would wish to be thy king!   855

XXXI

' But soft! what messenger of speed
Spurs hitherward his panting steed?
I guess his cognizance[1] afar —
What from our cousin, John of Mar?' —
' He prays, my liege, your sports keep bound   840
Within the safe and guarded ground:
For some foul purpose yet unknown, —
Most sure for evil to the throne, —
The outlawed chieftain, Roderick Dhu,
Has summoned his rebellious crew;   845
'Tis said, in James of Bothwell's aid
These loose banditti[2] stand arrayed.
The Earl of Mar this morn from Doune
To break their muster marched, and soon
Your grace will hear of battle fought;   850
But earnestly the Earl besought,
Till for such danger he provide,
With scanty train you will not ride.'

XXXII

' Thou warn'st me I have done amiss, —
I should have earlier looked to this: 855

[1] Coat-of-arms.   [2] Bandits, outlaws.

I lost [1] it in this bustling day.
— Retrace with speed thy former way;
Spare not for spoiling of [2] thy steed, —
The best of mine shall be thy meed.
Say to our faithful Lord of Mar,860
We do forbid the intended war:
Roderick, this morn, in single fight,
Was made our prisoner by a knight;
And Douglas hath himself and cause
Submitted to our kingdom's laws.865
The tidings of their leaders lost
Will soon dissolve the mountain host,
Nor would we that the vulgar [3] feel,
For their chief's crimes, avenging steel.
Bear Mar our message, Braco: fly!'—870
He turned his steed, — 'My liege, I hie, —
Yet ere I cross this lily lawn
I fear the broadswords will be drawn.'
The turf the flying courser spurned,
And to his towers the king returned.875

XXXIII

Ill with King James's mood that day
Suited gay feast and minstrel lay;
Soon were dismissed the courtly throng,
And soon cut short the festal song.
Nor less upon the saddened town880
The evening sunk in sorrow down.

[1] Forgot.[2] For fear of spoiling.[3] Common people.

The burghers spoke of civil jar,
Of rumoured feuds and mountain war,
Of Moray, Mar, and Roderick Dhu,
All up in arms:— the Douglas too,   885
They mourned him pent within the hold,
'Where stout Earl William was of old.'—
And there his word the speaker staid,
And finger on his lip he laid,
Or pointed to his dagger blade.   890
But jaded horsemen from the west
At evening to the castle pressed;
And busy talkers said they bore
Tidings of fight on Katrine's shore;
At noon the deadly fray begun,   895
And lasted till the set of sun.
Thus giddy rumour shook the town,
Till closed the Night her pennons[1] brown.

[1] Wings.

CANTO SIXTH

The Guard-room

I

'The sun, awakening, through the smoky **air**
　　Of the dark city casts a sullen glance,
Rousing each caitiff[1] to his task of care,
　　Of sinful man the sad inheritance;
Summoning revellers from the lagging dance,　　　　5
　　Scaring the prowling robber to his den;
Gilding on battled tower the warder's lance,
　　And warning student pale to leave his pen,
And yield his drowsy eyes to the kind nurse of men.

What various scenes, and, O! what scenes of woe,　10
　　Are witnessed by that red and struggling beam!
The fevered patient, from his pallet low,
　　Through crowded hospital beholds its stream;
The ruined maiden trembles at its gleam,
　　The debtor wakes to thought of gyve and jail,　15
The love-lorn wretch starts from tormenting dream;
　　The wakeful mother, by the glimmering pale,
Trims[2] her sick infant's couch, and soothes his feeble
　　　　wail.

II

　　At dawn the towers of Stirling rang
　　With soldier-step and weapon-clang,　　　　　20

---
[1] Wretch.　　　　　[2] Makes trim.

While drums, with rolling note, foretell
Relief to weary sentinel.
Through narrow loop and casement barred,
The sunbeams sought the Court of Guard,
And, struggling with the smoky air,   25
Deadened the torches' yellow glare.
In comfortless alliance shone
The lights through arch of blackened stone,
And showed wild shapes in garb of war,
Faces deformed with beard and scar,   30
All haggard from the midnight watch,
And fevered with the stern debauch;
For the oak table's massive board,
Flooded with wine, with fragments stored,
And beakers drained, and cups o'erthrown, 35
Showed in what sport the night had flown.
Some, weary, snored on floor and bench;
Some laboured still their thirst to quench;
Some, chilled with watching, spread their hands
O'er the huge chimney's dying brands,   40
While round them, or beside them flung,
At every step their harness[1] rung.

III

These drew not for their fields the sword,
Like tenants of a feudal lord,
Nor owned the patriarchal claim
Of chieftain in their leader's name;   45

[1] Armour.

Adventurers they, from far who roved,
To live by battle which they loved.
There the Italian's clouded face,
The swarthy Spaniard's there you trace;50
The mountain-loving Switzer there
More freely breathed in mountain-air:
The Fleming¹ there despised the soil
That paid so ill the labourer's toil;
Their rolls showed French and German name;55
And merry England's exiles came,
To share, with ill-concealed disdain,
Of Scotland's pay the scanty gain.
All brave in arms, well trained to wield
The heavy halberd,² brand, and shield;60
In camps licentious, wild, and bold;
In pillage fierce and uncontrolled;
And now, by holytide³ and feast,
From rules of discipline released.

IV

They held debate of bloody fray,65
Fought 'twixt Loch Katrine and Achray.
Fierce was their speech, and 'mid their words
Their hands oft grappled to their swords;
Nor sunk their tone to spare the ear
Of wounded comrades groaning near,70
Whose mangled limbs and bodies gored
Bore token of the mountain sword,

¹ Native of Flanders.   ² A kind of battle-ax.   ³ Holiday.

Though, neighbouring to the Court of Guard,
Their prayers and feverish wails were heard, —
Sad burden [1] to the ruffian joke,   75
And savage oath by fury spoke ! —
At length up-started John of Brent
A yeoman from the banks of Trent ;
A stranger to respect or fear,
In peace a chaser of the deer,   8o
In host a hardy mutineer,
But still the boldest of the crew,
When deed of danger was to do.
He grieved, that day, their games cut short,
And marred the dicer's brawling sport,   85
And shouted loud, ' Renew the bowl !
And, while a merry catch [2] I troll,[3]
Let each the buxom [4] chorus bear,
Like brethren of the brand and spear.'

V

SOLDIER'S SONG

' Our vicar still preaches that Peter and Poule [5]   90
Laid a swinging long curse on the bonny brown bowl,
That there's wrath and despair in the jolly black-jack,[6]
And the seven deadly sins in a flagon of sack[7] ;
Yet whoop, Barnaby ! off with thy liquor,
Drink upsees out,[8] and a fig for the vicar !   95

[1] Refrain.   [2] Song (round).   [3] Sing.   [4] Lively.   [5] Paul.
      [6] A kind of jug.   [7] Wine.   [8] Deeply.

'Our vicar he calls it damnation to sip
The ripe ruddy dew of a woman's dear lip,
Says that Beelzebub lurks in her kerchief so sly,
And Apollyon shoots darts from her merry black eye;
Yet whoop, Jack! kiss Gillian the quicker, 100
Till she bloom like a rose, and a fig for the vicar!

'Our vicar thus preaches—and why should he not?
For the dues of his cure[1] are the placket and pot[2];
And 'tis right of his office poor laymen to lurch,[3]
Who infringe the domains of our good Mother Church.
Yet whoop, bully-boys! off with your liquor, 106
Sweet Marjorie's the word, and a fig for the vicar!'

VI

The warder's challenge, heard without,
Staid in mid-roar the merry shout.
A soldier to the portal went,— 110
'Here is old Bertram, sirs, of Ghent;
And,—beat for jubilee the drum!
A maid and minstrel with him come.'
Bertram, a Fleming, grey and scarred,
Was entering now the Court of Guard, 115
A harper with him, and, in plaid
All muffled close, a mountain maid,
Who backward shrunk to 'scape the view
Of the loose scene and boisterous crew.

---

[1] Office, charge.   [2] Women and wine.   [3] Rob.

'What news?' they roared. — 'I only know   120
From noon till eve we fought with foe
As wild and as untamable
As the rude mountains where they dwell;
On both sides store¹ of blood is lost,
Nor much success can either boast.' —   125
'But whence thy captives, friend? such spoil
As theirs must needs reward thy toil.
Old dost thou wax,² and wars grow sharp;
Thou now hast glee-maiden³ and harp!
Get thee an ape, and trudge the land,   130
The leader of a juggler band.' —

VII

'No, comrade; — no such fortune mine.
After the fight, these sought our line,
That aged harper and the girl,
And, having audience of the Earl,   135
Mar bade I should purvey⁴ them steed,
And bring them hitherward with speed.
Forbear your mirth and rude alarm,
For none shall do them shame or harm.' —
'Hear ye his boast?' cried John of Brent,   140
Ever to strife and jangling⁵ bent;
'Shall he strike doe beside our lodge,
And yet the jealous niggard grudge
To pay the forester his fee?

¹ Plenty.   ² Grow.   ³ Song-girl.   ⁴ Furnish.   ⁵ Quarrelling.

I'll have my share, howe'er it be,   145
Despite of Moray, Mar, or thee.'
Bertram his forward step withstood;
And, burning in his vengeful mood,
Old Allan, though unfit for strife,
Laid hand upon his dagger-knife;   150
But Ellen boldly stepped between,
And dropped at once the tartan screen: —
So, from his morning cloud, appears
The sun of May, through summer tears.
The savage soldiery, amazed,   155
As on descended angel gazed;
Even hardy Brent, abashed and tamed,
Stood half admiring, half ashamed.

VIII

Boldly she spoke, — ' Soldiers, attend!
My father was the soldier's friend;   160
Cheered him in camps, in marches led,
And with him in the battle bled.
Not from the valiant or the strong
Should exile's daughter suffer wrong.' —
Answered De Brent, most forward still   165
In every feat or good or ill, —
' I shame me of the part I played;
And thou an outlaw's child, poor maid!
An outlaw I by forest laws,
And merry Needwood knows the cause.   170

Poor Rose, — if Rose be living now,' —
He wiped his iron eye and brow, —
'Must bear such age, I think, as thou. —
Hear ye, my mates ; — I go to call
The captain of our watch to hall :   175
There lies my halberd on the floor ;
And he that steps my halberd o'er,
To do the maid injurious part,
My shaft shall quiver in his heart ! —
Beware loose speech, or jesting rough :   180
Ye all know John de Brent.   Enough.'

IX

Their captain came, a gallant young, —
(Of Tullibardine's house he sprung,)
Nor wore he yet the spurs of knight ;
Gay was his mien, his humour light,   185
And, though by courtesy controlled,
Forward his speech, his bearing bold.
The high-born maiden ill could brook
The scanning of his curious look
And dauntless eye ; — and yet, in sooth,   190
Young Lewis was a generous youth ;
But Ellen's lovely face and mien,
Ill suited to the garb and scene,
Might lightly bear construction strange,
And give loose fancy scope to range.   195
'Welcome to Stirling towers, fair maid !
Come ye to seek a champion's aid,

On palfrey white, with harper hoar,
Like errant damosel[1] of yore?
Does thy high quest a knight require,　　200
Or may the venture suit a squire?'—
Her dark eye flashed;—she paused and sighed,—
'O what have I to do with pride ì—
Through scenes of sorrow, shame, and strife,
A suppliant for a father's life,　　205
I crave an audience of the king.
Behold, to back my suit, a ring,
The royal pledge of grateful claims,
Given by the monarch to Fitz-James.'

X

The signet-ring young Lewis took,　　210
With deep respect and altered look;
And said—'This ring our duties own;
And pardon, if to worth unknown,
In semblance mean[2] obscurely veiled,
Lady, in aught my folly failed.　　215
Soon as the day flings wide his gates,
The king shall know what suitor waits.
Please you, meanwhile, in fitting bower
Repose you till his waking hour;
Female attendance shall obey　　220
Your hest, for service or array.
Permit I marshal you the way.'

---

[1] Wandering maiden.　　　　[2] Lowly appearance.

But, ere she followed, with the grace
And open bounty of her race,
She bade her slender purse be shared   225
Among the soldiers of the guard.
The rest with thanks their guerdon took;
But Brent, with shy and awkward look,
On the reluctant maiden's hold
Forced bluntly back the proffered gold; —   230
'Forgive a haughty English heart,
And O forget its ruder part!
The vacant purse shall be my share,
Which in my barret-cap [1] I'll bear,
Perchance, in jeopardy of war,   235
Where gayer crests may keep afar.'
With thanks — 'twas all she could — the maid
His rugged courtesy repaid.

XI

When Ellen forth with Lewis went,
Allan made suit to John of Brent: —   240
'My lady safe, O let your grace
Give me to see my master's face!
His minstrel I, — to share his doom
Bound from the cradle to the tomb.
Tenth in descent, since first my sires   245
Waked for his noble house their lyres,
Nor one of all the race was known
But prized its weal above their own.

[1] Military cap.

With the chief's birth begins our care;
Our harp must soothe the infant heir, 250
Teach the youth tales of fight, and grace
His earliest feat of field or chase;
In peace, in war, our rank we keep,
We cheer his board, we soothe his sleep,
Nor leave him till we pour our verse — 255
A doleful tribute! — o'er his hearse.
Then let me share his captive lot;
It is my right — deny it not!' —
'Little we reck,' said John of Brent,
'We Southern men, of long descent; 260
Nor wot[1] we how a name — a word —
Makes clansmen vassals to a lord:
Yet kind my noble landlord's part, —
God bless the house of Beaudesert!
And, but I loved to drive the deer 265
More than to guide the labouring steer,
I had not dwelt an outcast here.
Come, good old minstrel, follow me;
Thy lord and chieftain shalt thou see.'

XII

Then from a rusted iron hook 270
A bunch of ponderous keys he took,
Lighted a torch, and Allan led
Through grated arch and passage dread.

[1] Know.

Portals they passed, where, deep within,
Spoke prisoner's moan, and fetters' din ;   275
Through rugged vaults, where, loosely stored,
Lay wheel, and ax, and headsman's sword,
And many an hideous engine grim
For wrenching joint and crushing limb,
By artists formed who deemed it shame   280
And sin to give their work a name.
They halted at a low-browed porch,
And Brent to Allan gave the torch,
While bolt and chain he backward rolled,
And made the bar unhasp its hold.   285
They entered : — 'twas a prison room
Of stern security and gloom,
Yet not a dungeon ; for the day
Through lofty gratings found its way,
And rude and antique garniture   290
Decked the sad walls and oaken floor ;
Such as the rugged days of old
Deemed fit for captive noble's hold.
' Here,' said De Brent, ' thou mayst remain
Till the leech [1] visit him again.   295
Strict is his charge, the warders tell,
To tend the noble prisoner well.'
Retiring then, the bolt he drew,
And the lock's murmurs growled anew.
Roused at the sound, from lowly bed   300
A captive feebly raised his head ;

[1] Physician.

The wondering minstrel looked, and knew —
Not his dear lord, but Roderick Dhu!
For, come from where Clan-Alpine fought,
They, erring, deemed the chief he sought.   305

XIII

As the tall ship, whose lofty prore [1]
Shall never stem the billows more,
Deserted by her gallant band,
Amid the breakers lies astrand,[2] —
So, on his couch, lay Roderick Dhu!   310
And oft his fevered limbs he threw
In toss abrupt, as when her sides
Lie rocking in the advancing tides,
That shake her frame with ceaseless beat,
Yet cannot heave her from her seat; —   315
O, how unlike her course on sea!
Or his free step on hill and lea! —
Soon as the minstrel he could scan,
'What of thy lady? — of my clan? —
My mother? — Douglas? — tell me all? —   320
Have they been ruined in my fall?
Ah, yes! or wherefore art thou here?
Yet speak, — speak boldly, — do not fear.' —
(For Allan, who his mood well knew,
Was choked with grief and terror too.)   325
'Who fought? — who fled? — Old man, be brief; —
Some might — for they had lost their chief.

---

[1] Prow.   [2] Stranded.

Who basely live? — who bravely died?'—
'O, calm thee, Chief!' the minstrel cried;
'Ellen is safe;'—'For that, thank Heaven!'—
'And hopes are for the Douglas given;—   331
The Lady Margaret, too, is well;
And, for thy clan,—on field or fell,
Has never harp of minstrel told
Of combat fought so true and bold.   335
Thy stately Pine is yet unbent,
Though many a goodly bough is rent.'

XIV

The chieftain reared his form on high,
And fever's fire was in his eye;
But ghastly, pale, and livid streaks   340
Chequered his swarthy brow and cheeks.
—'Hark, minstrel! I have heard thee play,
With measure bold, on festal day,
In yon lone isle,—again where ne'er
Shall harper play, or warrior hear!—   345
That stirring air that peals on high
O'er Dermid's race our victory.—
Strike it!—and then, (for well thou canst)
Free from thy minstrel-spirit glanced,[1]
Fling me the picture of the fight,   350
When met my clan the Saxon might.
I'll listen, till my fancy hears
The clang of swords, the crash of spears!

[1] Flashed.

These grates, these walls, shall vanish then,
For the fair field of fighting men,   355
And my free spirit burst away,
As if it soared from battle-fray.'
The trembling bard with awe obeyed, —
Slow on the harp his hand he laid;
But soon remembrance of the sight   360
He witnessed from the mountain's height,
With what old Bertram told at night,
Awakened the full power of song,
And bore him in career along; —
As shallop launched on river's tide,   365
That slow and fearful leaves the side,
But, when it feels the middle stream,
Drives downward swift as lightning's beam.

XV

BATTLE OF BEAL' AN DUINE

'The minstrel came once more to view
The eastern ridge of Benvenue,   370
For, ere he parted, he would say
Farewell to lovely Loch Achray —
Where shall he find, in foreign land,
So lone a lake, so sweet a strand!
    There is no breeze upon the fern,   375
      Nor ripple on the lake,
  Upon her eyry nods the erne,[1]
      The deer has sought the brake;

[1] Eagle.

The small birds will not sing aloud,
  The springing trout lies still, 380
So darkly glooms yon thunder-cloud,
That swathes, as with a purple shroud,
  Benledi's distant hill.
Is it the thunder's solemn sound
  That mutters deep and dread, 385
Or echoes from the groaning ground
  The warrior's measured tread?
Is it the lightning's quivering glance
  That on the thicket streams,
Or do they flash on spear and lance 390
  The sun's retiring beams?
I see the dagger-crest of Mar,
I see the Moray's silver star,
Wave o'er the cloud of Saxon war,
That up the lake comes winding far! 395
  To hero bound for battle-strife,
    Or bard of martial lay,
  'Twere worth ten years of peaceful life,
    One glance at their array!

XVI

¹ Their light-armed archers far and near 400
  Surveyed the tangled ground;
Their centre ranks, with pike and spear,
  A twilight forest frowned;
Their barded¹ horsemen, in the rear,

¹ Armoured.

The stern battalia[1] crowned.   405
No cymbal clashed, no clarion rang,
  Still were the pipe and drum;
Save heavy tread, and armour's clang,
  The sullen march was dumb.
There breathed no wind their crests to shake,
  Or wave their flags abroad;   411
Scarce the frail aspen seemed to quake,
  That shadowed o'er their road.
Their vaward[2] scouts no tidings bring,
  Can rouse no lurking foe,   415
Nor spy a trace of living thing,
  Save when they stirred the roe;
The host moves like a deep-sea wave,
Where rise no rocks its pride to brave,
  High-swelling, dark, and slow.   420
The lake is passed, and now they gain
A narrow and a broken plain,
Before the Trosachs' rugged jaws;
And here the horse and spearmen pause,
While, to explore the dangerous glen,   425
Dive through the pass the archer-men.

XVII

At once there rose so wild a yell
Within that dark and narrow dell,
As[3] all the fiends, from heaven that fell,
Had pealed the banner-cry of hell!   430

   [1] Army.   [2] Vanguard.   [3] As if.

Forth from the pass in tumult driven,
Like chaff before the wind of heaven,
　　The archery appear;
For life! for life! their flight they ply —
And shriek, and shout, and battle-cry,　　　　**435**
And plaids and bonnets waving high,
And broadswords flashing to the sky,
　　Are maddening in the rear.
Onward they drive, in dreadful race,
　　Pursuers and pursued;　　　　　　　**440**
Before that tide of flight and chase,
How shall it keep its rooted place,
　　The spearmen's twilight wood? —
"Down, down," cried Mar, "your lances down!
　　Bear back both friend and foe!" —　　**445**
Like reeds before the tempest's frown,
That serried grove of lances brown
　　At once lay levelled low;
And closely shouldering side to side,
The bristling ranks the onset bide. —　　**450**
"We'll quell the savage mountaineer,
　　As their tinchel[1] cows[2] the game!
They come as fleet as forest deer,
　　We'll drive them back as tame." —

XVIII

'Bearing before them, in their course,　　**455**
　　The relics[3] of the archer force,

---

[1] Circle of sportsmen.　　　[2] Overcomes.　　　[3] Remainder.

Like wave with crest of sparkling foam,
Right onward did Clan-Alpine come.
  Above the tide, each broadsword bright
  Was brandishing like beam of light,   460
    Each targe was dark below;
  And with the ocean's mighty swing,
  When heaving to the tempest's wing,
    They hurled them on the foe.
I heard the lance's shivering crash,   465
As when the whirlwind rends the ash;
I heard the broadsword's deadly clang,
As if an hundred anvils rang!
But Moray wheeled his rearward rank
Of horsemen on Clan-Alpine's flank,   470
    — "My banner-man, advance!
  I see," he cried, "their column shake. —
  Now, gallants! for your ladies' sake,
    Upon them with the lance!" —
The horsemen dashed among the rout,   475
  As deer break through the broom;
Their steeds are stout, their swords are out,
  They soon make lightsome room.
Clan-Alpine's best are backward borne —
  Where, where was Roderick then?   480
One blast upon his bugle-horn
  Were worth a thousand men!
And refluent[1] through the pass of fear
  The battle's tide was poured;

[1] Flowing back.

Vanished the Saxon's struggling spear,   485
   Vanished the mountain-sword,
As Bracklinn's chasm, so black and steep,
   Receives her roaring linn,[1]
As the dark caverns of the deep
   Suck the dark whirlpool in,   490
So did the deep and darksome pass
Devour the battle's mingled mass:
None linger now upon the plain,
Save those who ne'er shall fight again.

XIX

'Now westward rolls the battle's din,   495
That deep and doubling pass within.
— Minstrel, away! the work of fate
Is bearing on: its issue wait,
Where the rude Trosachs' dread defile
Opens on Katrine's lake and isle. —   500
Grey Benvenue I soon repassed,
Loch Katrine lay beneath me cast.
   The sun is set; — the clouds are met,
     The lowering scowl of heaven
   An inky hue of livid blue   505
     To the deep lake has given;
Strange gusts of wind from mountain glen
Swept o'er the lake, then sunk again.
I heeded not the eddying surge,
Mine eye but saw the Trosachs' gorge,   510

[1] Water-fall.

Mine ear but heard that sullen sound,
Which like an earthquake shook the ground,
And spoke the stern and desperate strife
That parts not but with parting life,
Seeming, to minstrel ear, to toll 515
The dirge of many a passing soul.
   Nearer it comes — the dim-wood glen
   The martial flood disgorged again,
     But not in mingled tide;
   The plaided warriors of the North 520
   High on the mountain thunder forth
     And overhang its side;
   While by the lake below appears
   The darkening cloud of Saxon spears.
At weary bay[1] each shattered band, 525
Eyeing their foemen, sternly stand;
Their banners stream like tattered sail,
That flings its fragments to the gale,
And broken arms and disarray
Marked the fell[2] havoc of the day. 530

XX

'Viewing the mountain's ridge askance,
The Saxon stood in sullen trance,
Till Moray pointed with his lance,
   And cried — "Behold yon isle! —
See! none are left to guard its strand, 535
But women weak, that wring the hand:

  [1] Weary, and at bay.   [2] Destructive.

'Tis there of yore the robber band
    Their booty wont to pile ; —
My purse, with bonnet-pieces [1] store,
To him will swim a bow-shot o'er,   540
And loose a shallop from the shore.
Lightly we'll tame the war-wolf then,
Lords of his mate, and brood, and den." —
Forth from the ranks a spearman sprung,
On earth his casque and corslet rung,   545
    He plunged him in the wave : —
All saw the deed — the purpose knew,
And to their clamours Benvenue
        A mingled echo gave ;
The Saxons shout, their mate to cheer,   550
The helpless females scream for fear,
And yells for rage the mountaineer.
'Twas then, as by the outcry riven,[2]
Poured down at once the lowering heaven ;
A whirlwind swept Loch Katrine's breast,   555
Her billows reared their snowy crest.
Well for the swimmer swelled they high,
To mar the Highland marksman's eye ;
For round him showered, 'mid rain and hail,
The vengeful arrows of the Gael. —   560
In vain — He nears the isle — and lo !
His hand is on a shallop's bow.
    — Just then a flash of lightning came,
It tinged the waves and strand with flame ; —

[1] Gold coins, showing the king bonneted.   [2] Shattered.

I marked Duncraggan's widowed dame, —   565
Behind an oak I saw her stand,
A naked dirk gleamed in her hand :
It darkened, — but, amid the moan
Of waves, I heard a dying groan ;
Another flash ! — the spearman floats   570
A weltering corse beside the boats,
And the stern matron o'er him stood,
Her hand and dagger streaming blood.

XXI

' "Revenge ! revenge !" the Saxons cried —
The Gaels' exulting shout replied.   575
Despite the elemental rage,
Again they hurried to engage ;
But, ere they closed in desperate fight,
Bloody with spurring came a knight,
Sprung from his horse, and, from a crag,   580
Waved 'twixt the hosts a milk-white flag.
Clarion and trumpet by his side
Rung forth a truce-note high and wide,
While, in the monarch's name, afar
A herald's voice forbade the war,   585
For Bothwell's lord, and Roderick bold,
Were both, he said, in captive hold.'
— But here the lay made sudden stand, —
The harp escaped the minstrel's hand ! —
Oft had he stolen a glance, to spy   590
How Roderick brooked his minstrelsy :

At first, the chieftain to the chime,[1]
With lifted hand, kept feeble time ;
That motion ceased, — yet feeling strong
Varied his look as changed the song ;　595
At length, no more his deafened ear
The minstrel melody can hear ;
His face grows sharp, — his hands are clenched
As if some pang his heart-strings wrenched ;
Set are his teeth, his fading eye　600
Is sternly fixed on vacancy ;
Thus, motionless and moanless, drew
His parting breath stout Roderick Dhu !—
Old Allan-Bane looked on aghast,
While grim and still his spirit passed :　605
But when he saw that life was fled,
He poured his wailing o'er the dead.

XXII

LAMENT

And art thou cold and lowly laid,
Thy foeman's dread, thy people's aid,
Breadalbane's boast, Clan-Alpine's shade !　610
For thee shall none a requiem say ?
— For thee, — who loved the minstrel's lay,
For thee, of Bothwell's house the stay,
The shelter of her exiled line.
E'en in this prison-house of thine,　615
I'll wail for Alpine's honoured Pine !

[1] Music.

What groans shall yonder valleys fill!
What shrieks of grief shall rend yon hill!
What tears of burning rage shall thrill,
When mourns thy tribe thy battles done,   620
Thy fall before the race was won,
Thy sword ungirt ere set of sun!
There breathes not clansman of thy line,
But would have given his life for thine. —
O woe for Alpine's honoured Pine!   625

'Sad was thy lot on mortal stage! —
The captive thrush may brook the cage,
The prisoned eagle dies for rage.
Brave spirit, do not scorn my strain!
And, when its notes awake again,   630
Even she, so long beloved in vain,
Shall with my harp her voice combine,
And mix her woe and tears with mine,
To wail Clan-Alpine's honoured Pine.' —

XXIII

Ellen, the while, with bursting heart,   635
Remained in lordly bower apart,
Where played, with many-coloured gleams,
Through storied pane the rising beams.
In vain on gilded roof they fall,
And lightened up a tapestried wall,   640
And for her use a menial train
A rich collation spread in vain.

The banquet proud, the chamber gay,
Scarce drew one curious glance astray;
Or, if she looked, 'twas but to say   645
With better omen dawned the day
In that lone isle, where waved on high
The dun-deer's hide for canopy;
Where oft her noble father shared
The simple meal her care prepared,   650
While Lufra, crouching by her side,
Her station claimed with jealous pride,
And Douglas, bent on woodland game,
Spoke of the chase to Malcolm Græme,
Whose answer, oft at random made,   655
The wandering of his thoughts betrayed.
Those who such simple joys have known
Are taught to prize them when they're gone.
But sudden, see, she lifts her head!
The window seeks with cautious tread.   660
What distant music has the power
To win her in this woeful hour?
'Twas from a turret that o'erhung
Her latticed bower, the strain was sung.

XXIV

LAY OF THE IMPRISONED HUNTSMAN

' My hawk is tired of perch and hood,   665
My idle greyhound loathes his food,
My horse is weary of his stall,
And I am sick of captive thrall.

I wish I were, as I have been,
Hunting the hart in forest green, 670
With bended bow and bloodhound free,
For that's the life is meet [1] for me.

'I hate to learn the ebb of time,
From yon dull steeple's drowsy chime,
Or mark it as the sunbeams crawl, 675
Inch after inch, along the wall.
The lark was wont my matins ring,
The sable rook my vespers sing;
These towers, although a king's they be,
Have not a hall of joy for me. 680

'No more at dawning morn I rise,
And sun myself in Ellen's eyes,
Drive the fleet deer the forest through,
And homeward wend with evening dew;
A blithesome welcome blithely meet, 685
And lay my trophies at her feet,
While fled the eve on wing of glee, —
That life is lost to love and me!'

XXV

The heart-sick lay was hardly said,
The listener had not turned her head, 690
It trickled still, the starting tear,
When light a footstep struck her ear,
And Snowdoun's graceful knight was near.

[1] Fitting.

She turned the hastier, lest again
The prisoner should renew his strain. —   695
'O welcome, brave Fitz-James!' she said;
'How may an almost orphan maid
Pay the deep debt' — 'O say not so!
To me no gratitude you owe.
Not mine, alas! the boon to give,   700
And bid thy noble father live;
I can but be thy guide, sweet maid,
With Scotland's king thy suit to aid.
No tyrant he, though ire and pride
May lay his better mood aside.   705
Come, Ellen, come! 'tis more than time —
He holds his court at morning prime.'[1]
With beating heart, and bosom wrung,
As to a brother's arm she clung:
Gently he dried the falling tear,   710
And gently whispered hope and cheer;
Her faltering steps half led, half staid,[2]
Through gallery fair and high arcade,
Till, at his touch, its wings of pride
A portal arch unfolded wide.   715

XXVI

Within 'twas brilliant all and light,
A thronging scene of figures bright;
It glowed on Ellen's dazzled sight,

---

[1] The first period of the morning.   [2] Supported.

As when the setting sun has given
Ten thousand hues to summer even, 720
And from their tissue fancy frames
Aërial knights and fairy dames.
Still by Fitz-James her footing staid;
A few faint steps she forward made,
Then slow her drooping head she raised, 725
And fearful round the presence[1] gazed;
For him she sought who owned this state,
The dreaded prince whose will was fate!—
She gazed on many a princely port[2]
Might well have ruled a royal court; 730
On many a splendid garb she gazed,
Then turned bewildered and amazed,
For all stood bare; and in the room
Fitz-James alone wore cap and plume.
To him each lady's look was lent; 735
On him each courtier's eye was bent;
Midst furs and silks and jewels sheen,
He stood, in simple Lincoln green,
The centre of the glittering ring,—
And Snowdoun's knight is Scotland's king! 740

XXVII

As wreath of snow on mountain-breast
Slides from the rock that gave it rest,
Poor Ellen glided from her stay,[3]

---

[1] Presence-chamber.   [2] *I.e.* one with princely bearing

[3] Support.

And at the monarch's feet she lay;
No word her choking voice commands, —   745
She showed the ring — she clasped her hands.
O, not a moment could he brook,
The generous prince, that suppliant look!
Gently he raised her; and, the while,
Checked with a glance the circle's smile;   750
Graceful, but grave, her brow he kissed,
And bade her terrors be dismissed: —
' Yes, Fair; the wandering poor Fitz-James
The fealty of Scotland claims.
To him thy woes, thy wishes, bring;   755
He will redeem his signet ring.
Ask nought for Douglas; yester even,
His prince and he have much forgiven:
Wrong hath he had from slanderous tongue —
I, from his rebel kinsmen, wrong.   760
We would not to the vulgar crowd
Yield what they craved with clamour loud;
Calmly we heard and judged his cause,
Our council aided, and our laws.
I stanched thy father's death-feud stern   765
With stout De Vaux and grey Glencairn;
And Bothwell's lord henceforth we own
The friend and bulwark of our throne. —
But, lovely infidel, how now?
What clouds thy misbelieving brow?   770
Lord James of Douglas, lend thine aid;
Thou must confirm this doubting maid.'

XXVIII

Then forth the noble Douglas sprung,
And on his neck his daughter hung.
The monarch drank, that happy hour,   775
The sweetest, holiest draught of Power, —
When it can say, with godlike voice,
Arise, sad Virtue, and rejoice !
Yet would not James the general eye
On nature's raptures long should pry ;   780
He stepped between — ' Nay, Douglas, nay,
Steal not my proselyte away !
The riddle 'tis my right to read,
That brought this happy chance to speed.[1]
Yes, Ellen, when disguised I stray   785
In life's more low but happier way,
'Tis under name which veils my power ;
Nor falsely veils — for Stirling's tower
Of yore the name of Snowdoun claims,
And Normans call me James Fitz-James.   790
Thus watch I o'er insulted laws,
Thus learn to right the injured cause.' —
Then, in a tone apart and low, —
' Ah, little traitress ! none must know
What idle dream, what lighter thought,   795
What vanity full dearly bought,
Joined to thine eye's dark witchcraft, drew
My spell-bound steps to Benvenue,

[1] Success.

In dangerous hour, and all but gave
Thy monarch's life to mountain glaive!' —   800
Aloud he spoke — 'Thou still dost hold
That little talisman of gold,
Pledge of my faith, Fitz-James's ring: —
What seeks fair Ellen of the king?'

XXIX

Full well the conscious maiden guessed   805
He probed the weakness of her breast;
But, with that consciousness, there came
A lightening of her fears for Græme,
And more she deemed the monarch's ire
Kindled 'gainst him who for her sire,   810
Rebellious broadsword boldly drew;
And, to her generous feeling true,
She craved the grace[1] of Roderick Dhu. —
'Forbear thy suit: — the King of kings
Alone can stay life's parting wings;   815
I know his heart, I know his hand,
Have shared his cheer, and proved his brand; —
My fairest earldom would I give
To bid Clan-Alpine's chieftain live! —
Hast thou no other boon to crave?   820
No other captive friend to save?'
Blushing, she turned her from the king,
And to the Douglas gave the ring,
As if she wished her sire to speak

[1] Pardon.

The suit that stained[1] her glowing cheek. —   825
'Nay, then, my pledge has lost its force,
And stubborn justice holds her course. —
Malcolm, come forth!' — and, at the word,
Down kneeled the Græme to Scotland's lord.
'For thee, rash youth, no suppliant sues,   830
From thee may Vengeance claim her dues,
Who, nurtured underneath our smile,
Hast paid our care by treacherous wile,
And sought, amid thy faithful clan,
A refuge for an outlawed man,   835
Dishonouring thus thy loyal name. —
Fetters and warder[2] for the Græme!' —
His chain of gold the king unstrung,
The links o'er Malcolm's neck he flung,
Then gently drew the glittering band,   840
And laid the clasp on Ellen's hand.

Harp of the North, farewell! The hills grow dark,
   On purple peaks a deeper shade descending;
In twilight copse the glow-worm lights her spark,
   The deer, half-seen, are to the covert wending.   845
Resume thy wizard elm! the fountain lending,
   And the wild breeze, thy wilder minstrelsy;
Thy numbers sweet with nature's vespers blending,
   With distant echo from the fold and lea,
And herd-boy's evening pipe, and hum of housing[3]
   bee.   850

[1] Caused to redden.   [2] Jailer.   [3] Returning to the hive.

Yet, once again, farewell, thou minstrel Harp!
   Yet, once again, forgive my feeble sway!
And little reck I of the censure sharp
   May idly cavil[1] at an idle lay.
Much have I owed thy strains on life's long way,   855
   Through secret woes the world has never known,
When on the weary night dawned wearier day,
   And bitterer was the grief devoured alone.
That I o'erlive such woes, Enchantress! is thine own.

Hark! as my lingering footsteps slow retire,   860
   Some Spirit of the Air has waked thy string!
'Tis now a seraph bold, with touch of fire —
   'Tis now the brush of fairy's frolic wing; —
Receding now, the dying numbers ring
   Fainter and fainter down the rugged dell —   865
And now the mountain breezes scarcely bring
   A wandering witch-note of the distant spell —
And now, 'tis silent all! — Enchantress, fare thee well!

[1] Find fault.

NOTES

CANTO I

1. The introduction to each canto of the poem is in the form of Spenserian stanzas (of nine lines each, the last being an alexandrine or twelve-syllable verse), which contrast pleasingly with the short couplets of the narrative parts. In this case we have an imaginative address to the "Harp of the North," the idealized poetic spirit of Scotland.

2. **St. Fillan** was a saint of the seventh century. At least two springs were dedicated to him.

14. **According pause** is a phrase used of pauses in music which permit accompanying music to be heard.

21. **Though scarce my skill command,** *i.e.* though my skill may scarcely be able to attain (subjunctive).

28. **The stag at eve,** etc. Robert Louis Stevenson calls this opening of the story "one of the most spirited and poetic in, literature."

29. **Monan.** A Scottish saint.

31. **Glenartney.** A valley (see map).

33. **Benvoirlich.** For this, and the other mountains of the poem, see the map. *Ben* is the Gaelic prefix meaning "mountain." Scott frequently uses geographical and other terms in the Gaelic language, — the tongue of the Celtic clans of the Highlands, closely connected with the speech of the other Celtic races in Ireland and Wales, and of course wholly distinct from the speech of the Germanic races (to which English belongs).

47. **Tainted gale,** *i.e.* the air in which he scents the hunters.

235

53. Uam-Var. "Ua-Var, as the name is pronounced, or more properly Uaigh-Mor, is a mountain to the northeast of the village of Callander, in Menteith, deriving its name, which signifies the great den, or cavern, from a sort of retreat among the rocks on the south side, said by tradition to have been the abode of a giant." (Scott.)

54. Opening. A hunting term applied to the hounds when :hey begin to bark on scenting the game.

89. Menteith. The region of the River Teith (see map).

112. Brigg (Bridge) **of Turk.** This crosses a stream near Loch Achray (see map).

131. That mountain high. Benvenue.

137. The death-wound. "When the stag turned to bay, the ancient hunter had the perilous task of going in upon, and killing or disabling the desperate animal. . . . The task was dangerous, and to be adventured upon wisely and warily, either by getting behind the stag while he was gazing on the hounds, or by watching an opportunity to gallop roundly in upon him and kill him with the sword." (Scott.)

145. Trosachs. On this pass see the Introduction, page 35.

147. Close couched. This of course refers to the deer, the participle agreeing with the noun implied in "*his* head."

163. The banks of Seine. King James had been in France in 1536.

197. Shinar's plain. See *Genesis* xi. 2–4.

297. Drop a bead, *i.e.* say a prayer.

353. Measured mood. Stately manner.

425. Slighting the petty need, *i.e.* making light of his smaller necessities, — such as want of food.

438. Couch was pulled. Compare the opening of strophe 33 below.

459. Eye intent. The Celts believed in a gift of divination or prophecy called "second sight." Scott says: "It is called in Gaelic *Taishitaraugh,* from *Taish,* an unreal or shadowy appearance; and those possessed of the faculty are called *Taishatrin*, which may be aptly translated visionaries."

464. Lincoln green. This cloth was the common dress of Lowland Scotch and English yeomen and hunters. Compare Canto IV, line 575.

525. Idæan. The ancient Mount Ida, near Troy, was famous for its vines.

528. Hardy plant could bear. Scott occasionally omits the relative pronoun, as here after "plant"; a common licence in Shakespeare's time.

573. Ferragus or Ascabart. Two giants of romantic legendry.

580. Though more than kindred. For explanation, see Canto II, lines 249–252.

585. All unasked. "The Highlanders, who carried hospitality to a punctilious excess, are said to have considered it churlish to ask a stranger his name or lineage before he had taken refreshment." (Scott.)

591. Knight of Snowdoun. See Canto VI, lines 788–790.

622. A harp. Scott quotes here an old author, who says: "They (the Highlanders) delight much in music, but chiefly in harps and clairschoes of their own fashion. The strings of the clairschoes are made of brass wire, and the strings of the harp of sinews; which strings they strike either with their nails, growing long, or else with an instrument appointed for that use. . . . They sing verses prettily compound, containing for the most part praises of valiant men." Later the harp gave way to the bagpipe.

729. That exiled race. See the Introduction, p. 28, on the exile of the Douglases.

CANTO II

7. A minstrel grey. The minstrel was a regular officer of each great Scottish family, and it was his special duty to compose and sing lyrics in commemoration of the deeds of his master's race and friends (see line 109).

28. Southern sky. The Lowland region.

100. Not so had, *i.e.* would have.

131. St. Modan. A Scotch abbot of the seventh century.

141. Bothwell. An ancient castle of the Douglases, on the banks of the Clyde.

159. Tweed to Spey. The Tweed is the southern boundary of Scotland, the Spey a river far to the north.

200. The Bleeding Heart. This was the symbol or cognizance of the Douglas family.

213. Clan-Alpine, *i.e.* the clan of Alpine, really a number of related clans, all claiming descent from an ancient king named McAlpine.

216. A Lennox foray. The land of the Lennox family bordered the southern end of Loch Lomond.

221. Holy-Rood. The palace called Holyrood (still standing), in Edinburgh.

236. Dispensation sought. The permission of the Pope for the marriage of cousins.

260. Maronnan's cell. A chapel at the eastern end of Loch Lomond.

270. Bracklinn. "This beautiful cascade is on the Keltie, a mile from Callander. The height of the fall is fifty feet." (Scott.)

306. Tine-man. A nickname of Archibald, the third Earl of Douglas, who "was so unfortunate in all his enterprises, that he acquired the epithet of 'tine-man,' because he *tined*, or lost, his followers in every battle which he fought." (Scott.)

308. Border spears, etc. Douglas was concerned with Percy (Hotspur) in rebellion against Henry IV.

309. Self-unscabbarded. See Canto I, line 537.

319. Beltane. May-day, a Celtic festival in honour of the sun, which was called "Beal-tein," or "fire of Beal."

335. Glengyle. A valley at the northwestern end of Loch Katrine.

363. Thrilling sounds. Scott quotes from Dr. Beattie as follows: "A pibroch is a species of tune, peculiar, I think, to the Highlands and Western Isles of Scotland. It is performed on a bagpipe, and differs totally from all other music. Its rhythm is so irregular, and its notes, especially in the quick movement, so mixed and huddled together, that a stranger finds it impossible to reconcile his ear to it, so as to perceive its modulation. Some of these pibrochs, being intended to represent a battle, begin with a grave motion, resembling a march; then gradually quicken into the onset; run off with noisy confusion, and turbulent rapidity, to imitate the conflict and pursuit; then swell into a few flourishes of triumphant joy; and perhaps close with the wild and slow wailings of a funeral procession."

408. Roderigh Vich Alpine dhu. "Besides his ordinary name and surname, which were chiefly used in the intercourse with the Lowlands, every Highland chief had an epithet expressive of his patriarchal dignity as head of the clan. . . . But besides this title, which belonged to his office and dignity, the chieftain had usually another peculiar to himself, which distinguished him from the chieftains of the same race. This was sometimes derived from complexion, as *dhu* or *roy;* sometimes from size, as *beg* or *more;* at other times, from some peculiar exploit, or from some peculiarity of habit or appearance. The line of the text therefore signifies:

Black Roderick, the descendant of Alpine.

"The song itself is intended as an imitation of the *jorrams*, or boat songs of the Highlanders, which were usually composed in honour of a favourite chief. They are so adapted as to keep time with the sweep of the oars, and it is easy to distinguish between those intended to be sung to the oars of a galley, where the stroke is lengthened and doubled, as it were, and those which were timed to the rowers of an ordinary boat." (Scott.)

416. Menteith and Breadalbane. On Menteith see Canto I, line 89. The Breadalbane country was north of Loch Lomond.

419. Glen Fruin. This, and the names mentioned just below, are localities in the Loch Lomond region. Bannochar was a castle. Scott says, "The Lennox, as the district is called which encircles the lower extremity of Loch Lomond, was peculiarly exposed to the incursions of the mountaineers, who inhabited the inaccessible fastnesses at the upper end of the lake, and the neighbouring district of Loch Katrine."

426. Leven-Glen. The valley of the Leven, flowing from Loch Lomond to the Clyde.

498. Bloody field. The border war of 1388.

504. Waned crescent. The crescent was the badge of the Buccleuch family, and is represented as waning with their defeat in an attempt to restore the king.

506. Blantyre. A priory near Bothwell Castle.

525. Unhooded. The head of the falcon was ordinarily kept covered or hooded, except when it was released to fly after game.

541. Ptarmigan. A white bird.

571. Reft, etc., *i.e.* all of my original self that is left would be taken away with the pleasure of the chase.

574. Glenfinlas. A valley (see map).

583. Strath-Endrick. A valley southeast of Loch Lomond.

619. In bloody toils. "In 1529 James V made a convention at Edinburgh for the purpose of considering the best mode of quelling the Border robbers. . . . He assembled a flying army of ten thousand men, consisting of his principal nobility and their followers, who were directed to bring their hawks and dogs with them, that the monarch might refresh himself with sport during the intervals of military execution. With this array he swept through Ettrick Forest, where he hanged over the gate of his own castle Piers Cockburn of Henderland, who had prepared, according to tradition, a feast for his reception. . . . But the most noted victim of justice, during that expedition, was John Armstrong of Gilnockie, famous in Scottish song, who, confiding in his own supposed innocence, met the king with a retinue of 36 persons, all of whom were hanged at Carlenrig." (Scott.)

623–626. Meggat, etc. Of these rivers the Ettrick and Teviot are branches of the Tweed, Yarrow is a branch of the Ettrick, and the Meggat of Yarrow.

678. Links of Forth. The windings of the Forth east of Stirling.

679. Stirling's porch, *i.e.* at the entrance of the castle.

783. Death had been, *i.e.* would have resulted.

809. His henchman. Scott quotes a writer on Scotland as saying of the henchman: "This officer is a sort of secretary, and is to be ready, upon all occasions, to venture his life in defence of his master; and at drinking-bouts he stands behind his seat, at his haunch, from which his title is derived, and watches the conversation, to see if any one offends his patron."

831. The Fiery Cross. The call to arms (see next canto).

847. Holds in ward. See line 613.

860. Then . . . tide. Scott once wrote to a friend concerning this part of the story: "You must know this Malcom Graeme was a great plague to me from the beginning. You ladies can hardly comprehend how very stupid lovers are to everybody but mistresses. I gave him that dip in the lake by way of making him do something; but wet or dry I could make nothing of him. His insignificance is the greatest defect among many others in the poem; but the canvas was not broad enough to include him, considering I had to group the king, Roderick, and Douglas." Is this criticism just?

CANTO III

18. Fiery Cross. "When a chieftain designed to summon his clan upon any sudden or important emergency, he slew a goat, and making a cross of any light wood, seared its extremities in the fire, and extinguished them in the blood of the animal. . . . It was delivered to a swift and trusty messenger, who ran full speed with it to the next hamlet, where he presented it to the principal person, with a single word, implying the place of rendezvous. He who received the symbol was bound to send it forward, with equal dispatch, to the next village ; and thus it passed with incredible celerity through all the district which owed allegiance to the chief. . . . At sight of the Fiery Cross, every man, from sixteen years old to sixty, capable of bearing arms, was obliged instantly to repair, in his best arms and accoutrements, to the place of rendezvous. He who failed to appear suffered the extremities of fire and sword, which were emblematically denounced to the disobedient by the bloody and burnt marks upon this warlike signal." (Scott.)

74. Benharrow. A mountain at the northern end of Loch Lomond.

81. The hallowed creed, *i.e.* Christianity. Old Celtic (heathen) superstitions were actually mingled, among the Highlanders, with the teachings of the church. The **Druid** (line 76) was the early Celtic priest.

91. Of Brian . . . told. This legend of the birth of Brian Scott tells us is not his own invention, but was taken from a collection of Scottish antiquities.

116. Virgin snood. "The snood, or riband, with which a Scottish lass braided her hair, . . . was exchanged for the *curch, toy,* or coif, when she passed, by marriage, into the matron state." (Scott.)

138. Sable-lettered page. The "black letter" books of the early period of printing, in the type now called "Old English."

154. River Demon. "It was a natural attribute of such a character as the supposed hermit, that he should credit the numerous superstitions with which the minds of ordinary Highlanders are almost always imbued. A few of these are slightly alluded to in this stanza. The River Demon, or River-horse, for it is that form which he commonly assumes, is the Kelpy of the Lowlands, an evil and malicious spirit, delighting to forebode and to witness calamity.

... **The 'noontide hag'** (line 156), called in Gaelic *Glas-lich*, a tall, emaciated, gigantic female figure, is supposed in particular to haunt the district of Knoidart. ... The **Ben-Shie** (line 168) implies the female fairy whose lamentations were often supposed to precede the death of a chieftain of particular families. When she is visible, it is in the form of an old woman, with a blue mantle and streaming hair." (Scott.)

191. Inch-Cailliach. The Isle of Nuns or Old Women, at the lower end of Loch Lomond, where there was an ancient church-yard.

199. Notice the form of stanza introduced here, varied by shorter lines than the usual ones of eight syllables. In the earlier poem of *Marmion* Scott made much larger use of this.

253. Coir-Uriskin. See lines 620–634 below.

255. Beala-nam-bo. "The pass of the cattle," a glade on the opposite side of Benvenue from the Goblin Cave.

286. Lanrick Mead. A meadow near Loch Vennachar (see map).

300. Dun deer's hide, *i.e.* the leather "brogue" or buskin of the Highlander.

369. Coronach. "The Coronach of the Highlanders ... was a wild expression of lamentation, poured forth by the mourners over the body of a departed friend. When the words of it were articulate, they expressed the praises of the deceased." (Scott.)

452. Benledi saw, etc. "Inspection of the provincial map of Perthshire, or any large map of Scotland, will trace the progress of the signal through the small district of lakes and mountains, which, in exercise of my poetical privilege, I have subjected to the authority of my imaginary chieftain, and which, at the period of my romance, was really occupied by a clan who claimed a descent from Alpine. ... The first stage of the Fiery Cross is to Dun-craggan, a place near the Brigg of Turk, where a short stream divides Loch Achray from Loch Vennachar. From thence it passes toward Callander, and then, turning to the left up the pass of Leny, is consigned to Norman at the Chapel of Saint Bride, which stood on a small and romantic knoll in the middle of the valley called Strath-Ire. Tombea and Arnandave, or Ardmandave, are names of places in the vicinity. The alarm is then supposed to pass along the Lake of Lubnaig, and through the various glens in the district of Balquidder, including the neighbouring tracts of Glenfinlas and Strath-Gartney." (Scott.)

485. Coif-clad dame. See note on line 116.

530. Sickening pang. An allusion to *Proverbs* xiii. 12.

570. Midnight blaze. "The heath of the Scottish moorlands is often set fire to, that the sheep may have the advantage of the young herbage produced, in room of the tough old heather plants. This custom (execrated by sportsmen) produces occasionally the most beautiful nocturnal appearances." (Scott.)

580. Balvaig. The stream connecting Loch Lubnaig and Loch Voil.

583. Each man might claim. "Who" is omitted. See note on Canto I, line 528.

599. By his chieftain's hand. "The deep and implicit respect paid by the Highland clansmen to their chief, rendered this both a common and a solemn oath." (Scott.)

607. Rednoch. A castle north of Lake Menteith.

608. Cardross. A castle on the Clyde.

609. Duchray. A castle south of Loch Ard.

622. Coir-nan-Uriskin. "This is a very steep and romantic hollow in the mountain of Benvenue, overhanging the southeastern extremity of Loch Katrine. It is surrounded with stupendous rocks, and overshadowed with birch-trees, mingled with oaks. . . . . The name literally implies the Corri, or Den, of the Wild or Shaggy Men. Tradition has ascribed to the *Urisk*, who gives name to the cavern, a figure between a goat and a man." (Scott.)

713. Hymn. Notice how the whole song is based on two rhymes.

CANTO IV

19. Braes of Doune. The region on the north side of the Teith.

63. The Taghairm. "The Highlanders, like all rude people," says Scott, "had various superstitious modes of inquiring into futurity." In the case of the *Taghairm* "a person was wrapped up in the skin of a newly slain bullock, and deposited beside a waterfall, or at the bottom of a precipice, or in some other strange, wild, and unusual situation. . . . In this situation he revolved in his mind the question proposed; and whatever was impressed upon him by his exalted imagination, passed for the inspiration of the disembodied spirits who haunt these desolate recesses."

74. Beal 'maha. The "pass of the plain," east of Loch Lomond.

77. Dennan's Row. A settlement near the foot of Ben Lomond.

152. The Moray, *i.e.* the Earl of Moray. The reference is to the cognizance or device on arms and banners.

160. Earn. The district about Loch Earn, north of Ben Voirlich.

198. Red streamers of the North. The Aurora Borealis.

231. Cambus-Kenneth's fane. An abbey near Stirling.

261. The Ballad is a charming imitation of the old ballad form, both in the form of the stanza, the style, and the plot. The story is founded, Scott tells us, on a Danish ballad of the sixteenth century.

291. Richard. Scott imitates in this word the old "wrenched accent" often found at the end of a ballad line.

306. Fatal green. The fairies were believed to wear green, and to take offence if mortals assumed their colour.

340. 'Tis merry. Here the dwarf speaks.

371. Dunfermline. A town northwest of Edinburgh.

504. Female form. In a letter to a friend Scott once related the source of this character: "I wish I could give you an idea of the original, whom I really saw in the Pass of Glencoe many years ago. It is one of the wildest and most tremendous passes in the

Highlands, winding through huge masses of rock without a pile of verdure, and between mountains that seem rent asunder by an earthquake. This poor woman had placed herself in the wildest attitude imaginable, upon the very top of one of these huge frag- ments; she had scarce any covering but a tattered plaid, which left her arms, legs, and neck bare to the weather. Her long, shaggy, black hair was streaming backwards in the wind, and ex- posed a face rather wild and wasted than ugly, and bearing a very peculiar expression of frenzy. She had a handful of eagle's feathers in her hand."

523. **Better time,** *i.e.* better days.

531. **Allan.** This river, like the Devan (see next line), flows through Perthshire into the Forth.

575. **Lincoln green.** See note on Canto I, line 464.

594. **Of ten,** *i.e.* having ten branches on his antlers.

624. **Kindred ambush.** The same in meaning as "ambushed kin" in line 627.

745. **Space and law.** A reference to the rules of the hunt, under which the prey was given a start in the race.

751. **Come,** *i.e.* let Roderick come (subjunctive).

772. **Mighty augury.** Referring to lines 132, 133.

787. **Coilantogle's ford.** On the river Teith, where it flows from Loch Vennachar (see map).

CANTO V

108. **The Regent's court.** See Canto II, line 221. The Regent was the Duke of Albany (see line 124 below) who was called to the regency after the death of James IV.

263. **Doubt not aught,** etc., *i.e.* suspect nothing from this dis- play of my power.

300. **Ceaseless mines,** etc. "The torrent which discharges itself from Loch Vennachar . . . sweeps through a flat and exten- sive moor, called Bochastle. Upon a small eminence called the

Dun of Bochastle, and indeed on the plain itself, are some intrench-ments which have been thought Roman." (Scott.)

356. Carpet knight, *i.e.* a knight belonging by his character to the carpeted women's apartments.

383. Abroad, *i.e.* in France. See note on Canto I, line 163.

462. A fairer freight. See Canto IV, line 411.

485. Carhonie's hill. About a mile from Loch Vennachar.

490. Torry and Lendrick. These, and the following towns, are on the shore of the Teith, on the way to Stirling from Loch Vennachar.

534. Cambus-Kenneth. See Canto IV, line 231.

551. Sad and fatal mound. "An eminence on the northeast of the Castle, where state criminals were executed." (Scott.)

558. Franciscan steeple, *i.e.* of Greyfriars Church. The Fran-ciscan monks were those "of orders grey."

562. Morrice-dancers. The *morrice*, or *morris*, was a familiar dance, used at festivals, and often referred to in Shakespeare's time. See lines 611, 612 below.

564. Hold their sports. "Every burgh of Scotland of the least note, but more especially the considerable towns, had their solemn *play*, or festival, when feats of archery were exhibited, and prizes distributed to those who excelled in wrestling, hurling the bar, and the other gymnastic exercises of the period. Stirling, a usual place of royal residence, was not likely to be deficient in pomp upon such occasions, especially since James V was very partial to them. His ready participation in these popular amusements was one cause of his acquiring the title of the King of the Commons. . . . The usual prize to the best shooter was a silver arrow." (Scott.)

603. Hostage for their clan, *i.e.* held as guarantee against misbehaviour by their clan.

614. Robin Hood. "The exhibition of this renowned outlaw and his band was a favourite frolic at such festivals." (Scott.)

642. On the source of this part of the story, see the Introduction, page 28.

660. The Ladies' Rock. A point below Stirling Castle, formerly used for viewing games.

720. Stifled wrath. This passage is interestingly suggestive of Scott's own fondness for dogs, which was shown in all his writings so clearly that it was used as one of the evidences for the authorship of the Waverley Novels.

887. Earl William. The Douglas who was stabbed by James II in Stirling.

CANTO VI

47. Adventurers they. "The Scottish armies consisted chiefly of the nobility and barons, with their vassals, who held lands under them for military service by themselves and their tenants. . . . James V seems first to have introduced . . . the service of a small number of mercenaries, who formed a body-guard, called the Foot-Band." (Scott.)

53. Despised the soil. The soil of Flanders being noted for fertility.

78. Trent. A river of England.

95. Upsees out. A bit of Dutch drinking slang, more commonly found in the form "upsee" or "upsey."

99. Apollyon. Like Beelzebub, the name of a chief among evil spirits.

103. Dues of his cure. A jocose allusion to the freedom from restraint which the clergy, a privileged order, could exercise when they chose.

131. Juggler band. "The *jongleurs*, or jugglers, . . . used to call in the aid of various assistants, to render these performances as captivating as possible. The glee-maiden was a necessary attendant. Her duty was tumbling and dancing." (Scott.)

152. Tartan screen. The "plaid" of line 116.

170. Needwood. An English forest belonging to royalty.

183. Tullibardine. A seat of the Murray family, near Stirling.

199. Errant damosel. An allusion to the distressed ladies who figured in many old romances.

222. Permit I. *That* is omitted; *marshal* is subjunctive.

347. Dermid's race. Dermid was an ancient Celtic king.

363. Power of song. The minstrels were supposed to be able to extemporize on occasion.

369. Battle of Beal' an Duine. "A skirmish actually took place at a pass thus called in the Trosachs, and closed with the remarkable incident mentioned in the text. It was greatly posterior in date to the reign of James V." (Scott.) Scott goes on to tell how the women and children of the region took refuge, during the time of the raids of Cromwell's soldiers, on the island described in the first canto of the poem, and how a soldier who attempted to swim to it from the mainland was killed by one of the women.

452. Tinchel. This was "a circle of sportsmen, who, by surrounding a great space, and gradually narrowing, brought immense quantities of deer together, which usually made desperate efforts to break through the *Tinchel.*" (Scott.)

487. Bracklinn. See Canto II, line 270.

530. In connection with this description of the battle, Lockhart tells an interesting incident which he says Scott took special pride in relating. When a presentation copy of *The Lady of the Lake* reached Sir Adam Ferguson, an army officer who was an old friend of the poet, " he was posted with his company on a point of ground exposed to the enemy's artillery; somewhere, no doubt, on the lines of Torres Vedras. The men were ordered to lie prostrate on the ground; while they kept that attitude, the captain, kneeling at their head, read aloud the description of the battle in Canto VI, and the listening soldiers only interrupted him by a joyous huzza, whenever the French shot struck the bank close above them."

665. Perch and hood, *i.e.* idleness. On the hood, see note on Canto II, line 525.

734. Wore cap and plume. For the source of this point in the story, see the anecdote of King James quoted in the Introduction, page 31.

838. Byron told Scott that the Prince Regent (afterward George IV) once said to him that he regarded Scott as "particularly the poet of princes, as they never appeared more fascinating than in *Marmion* and *The Lady of the Lake.*"

846. Wizard elm. See the opening of Canto I.

851. Farewell. Scott felt at the time that this would be his last important poem; and he describes the pleasure he has found in this form of writing. It was not his ambition to be a great poet; hence he does not care ("little reck I") for the severe judgement ("censure sharp") of critics. The first and third of these concluding Spenserian stanzas show Scott's serious lyrical art at a point of dignity and beauty which he rarely attained.